Writing Toward Home

Writing Toward Home

TALES AND LESSONS TO FIND YOUR WAY

Georgia Heard

HEINEMANN
Portsmouth, NH

Heinemann
A division of Reed Elsevier Inc.
361 Hanover Street
Portsmouth, NH 03801–3912

Offices and agents throughout the world

Every effort has been made to contact the copyright holders for permission to
reprint borrowed material where necessary. We regret any oversights that may
have occurred and would be happy to rectify them in future printings of this work.

Acknowledgments for borrowed material can be found on page 145.

Parts of "Beginnings" and earlier versions of "The Rumble Beneath My Feet," "The
Education of the Eye: Staring," "From an Onion to My Grandmother," and "Blind
Contour Drawing: Revision" were published in *Teacher Research: The Journal of Class-
room Inquiry* (University of Maine) 1, no. 2 (spring 1994).

Library of Congress Cataloging-in-Publication Data

Heard, Georgia.
    Writing toward home : tales and lessons to find your way / Georgia Heard.
        p. cm.
    Includes bibliographical references.
    ISBN 0–435–08124–1
    1. English language–Rhetoric. 2. Creative writing.
    3. Autobiography. 4. Authorship. I. Title.
    PE1408.H4357 1995
    808'.02–dc20   95-11031
                                         CIP

Editor: Toby Gordon
Copy Editor: Alan Huisman
Production: Vicki Kasabian
Text design: Jenny Jensen Greenleaf
Cover design: Judy Arisman
Cover painting: "Suffolk Street Barn," by Georgia Heard,
in the collection of Sean T. P. Sullivan

Printed in the United States of America on acid-free paper
03   02   VP   10

To those whose voices have been silent

CONTENTS

Contents

Contents

ACKNOWLEDGMENTS

I'VE SEEN your faces. They are like mine: hungry for telling, for truth, for courage, for the energy and time to re-create our worlds. Tired—but we know there is a volcano, a waterfall, a river inside us, if we can only find it.

Writing is made of voices. Our single voices may seem to be lost in the bitter wind. But if we listen hard enough we can hear hundreds of other voices trying to sing like us. Like threads weaving a cloth. Like the constellation patterns we draw to connect stars. Voices who have never dared sing before.

As I've traveled to towns and cities around this country to talk and teach writing, I've heard you. You have given me a gift: voices to listen to, to weave with my own. There is no song unless we sing together.

Here are some of the people whose voices have sustained me:

Suzanne Gardinier, singer extraordinaire, without whom my world would be an infinitely more somber and silent place; Marie Howe, whose voice I've depended on, on the phone, every other day, for the past thirteen years; Bonnie

Uslianer, companion on many journeys. All three have given me speakable joy.

Many thanks to the hardworking people in my writing and teaching community, including Lucy Calkins, who through our dialogue on Amsterdam Avenue helped me find my own voice as a teacher; Shelley Harwayne, whose support continues to be invaluable; Don Graves, spinner of stories, wisdom, and more recently, poems; Irene Tully, who saw the first drafts of this book, whooped and hollered, and helped me keep going; Jason Shinder, whose careful reading helped me resee many parts of the book; and the many others around the country, some I've met only briefly, who have inspired me with the courage of their voices—including my friends in Arizona, who have taught me the delicate ways of the desert; in Hawai'i, who teach me the Aloha spirit; in Denver, who have shown me mountains of inspiration; on the east end of Long Island, who have given me the gifts of comradeship and home; and in New York City, my other home, who teach me about perseverance, tenacity, and love.

Thanks to all the people at Heinemann, including Toby Gordon, my editor, whose enthusiasm from the very beginning helped my words flow, and Karen Hiller (before her, Leslie Schwarz), my speaking agent, who sends me to towns and cities all over the country. Special thanks to Vicki Kasabian, Alan Huisman, Jenny Jensen Greenleaf, and Judy Arisman.

My gratitude to each one of you for helping to sustain me.

The moon and sun are eternal travelers. Even the years wander on. A lifetime adrift in a boat, or in old age leading a tired horse into the years, ending is a journey, and the journey itself is home.

—BASHŌ

Beginnings

I

HOME IS a blueprint of memory. I can draw it for you. Exactly which path went where. Where the creek curved. Where my sisters' pet ducks are buried. Alexandria, Virginia. Thirty miles outside Washington, D.C. A place we moved to when I was eight, from Germany, where my father was stationed. Home is the smell of the wet undersides of leaves behind our house—an earthy rotting acrid smell—and the shadow patches of cool that crossed my face like cobwebs as I ran through the woods. It's the smell of creek crayfish and thick mud after a storm, it's jumping on rocks over the creek, sometimes getting my sneakers wet, it's seeking the hiding crayfish. It's the cool of the backyard in late afternoon. Laddie's ticks. The gutters rushing with rain during a storm. The streetlight buzzing on and the bugs speeding around it like I imagine the planets orbiting around our sun. Something known like breath. Skin is a kind of home.

Germany is a more distant home, although I see some things vividly there: a loving Tante and Oncle who mixed raw eggs with sugar in a glass for me to drink and fortify myself for school, Tante Ellie who sang lullabies to me at bedtime with her clear silver bird voice. I have fewer memories of that home. But it was a safe nest.

Home is what can be recalled without effort—so that sometimes we think, oh, that can't be important. Memories are the blueprints of home. A memoir is a home built from those blueprints. Finding home is crucial to the act of writing. Begin here. With what you know. With the tales you've told dozens of times to friends or a spouse or a lover. With the map you've already made in your heart. That's where the real home is: inside. If we carry that home with us all the time, we'll be able to take more risks. We can leave on wild excursions, knowing we'll return.

II

For my thirty-fifth birthday my friend Bonnie gave me a talking stick: a stick that storytellers sometimes hold in their hands as they tell stories. A woman who lives in a yurt in Wyoming crafted it after Bonnie had told her about my life. On top of the smoothly polished but craggy stick sits a hand-painted stone carving of Raven Man. At first he is a little scary to look at: deep scars run down the length of his back, his skin is burned, his hands are gesturing, and his mouth open, speaking—telling stories. The artist told Bonnie: Raven Man travels all over the world telling stories. One night he and a bunch of friends were sitting around a fire, and he became excited; he was gesturing as he was telling a story and suddenly fell into the fire. He was badly burned but jumped out and soon continued to speak. Despite being burned, he is still speaking.

When I opened Bonnie's present, I immediately recognized myself in Raven Man. My flesh is not burned and scarred, but the way he looks resembles the way I have felt inside at times as I try to write the truth.

All writers fall in and out of the fire. We all have scars. Writing is not easy. It is a journey over rugged terrain of saguaro and prickly pear and then, with any luck, into valleys of still water and lush green.

Last year, right before I began this book, I stopped writing—for good, I thought. Writing was too dry; I wanted more moisture in my life. So I started to paint again, after a hiatus of ten years. I had been working on a memoir and had reached a point of frustration; I couldn't go any further. I put the book away. This time I would not jump out of the fire. This time I would never write again. Three months later, I began this book.

Throughout the country I meet people like myself who at some point in their lives decided to stop speaking—to stop telling their stories, to remain silent. Now they are writing in a workshop for the first time since college or high school, their voices shaky with beginning, angry with realized betrayals, or strong with defiance. As their writing teacher, my job is to try to help them speak again. To help them trust their own voices again. As a writer, my job is to keep walking out of the fire of silence myself, to keep telling the story of falling in and of climbing out again, to let my voice sing.

Querencia

A FEW summers ago I experienced my first—and last—bullfight, in a small French town near the Spanish border, where Picasso once lived. When the gate to the ring opened, the beautiful, confused bull burst in like wind, radiating power as he circled amid the shouts of the spectators. The matadors hid behind walls like scared children, studying the bull carefully. The banderillero approached on his horse and pierced the bull's neck with the banderillas—barbed swords. The swords hung from the bull; blood streamed down his shoulders. It was then I learned about *querencia*.

In Spanish, *querencia* describes a place where one feels safe, a place from which one's strength of character is drawn, a place where one feels at home. It comes from the verb *querer*, which means to desire, to want.

The wounded bull retreated to a spot to the left of the gate through which he had entered, to rest, it seemed. He had found his *querencia:* a place where he felt safe and was therefore at his most dangerous. The matador tries not to let the bull find this place, because it increases the danger to himself. For the bull, it is a place where he believes he can survive this unfair game. Unfortunately and cruelly, he almost never does. It is said that if the same bull were to fight more than once in the ring, every matador would die; once an animal learns the game and stands in his power, he cannot be defeated.

Animals have *querencia* by instinct. The golden plover knows every year where to fly when it migrates. Rattlesnakes know by the temperature when to lie dormant. In winter, sparrows and chickadees know where their food is and return to the same spot again and again. *Querencia* is a matter of survival. A nest, a mole's tunnel, is *querencia*.

Humans have *querencia*, too. We know where we feel most at home. Our bodies tell us, if we listen. There are certain seasons during which we feel more at ease. Certain times of day when we feel safe and more relaxed. Certain climates. Terrain. Even the clothes we wear make us feel more at home.

When I meet people I like to ask them what their *querencia* is. Some know immediately: mountains, the city, near the ocean. But many don't know. Having a sense of where we feel most at home is a way of keeping grounded; it can give us that sense of rootedness and safety. Some people's *querencia* is linked with nature: the sound of wind in the pines, the call of a loon, the salty smell of the ocean. Some feel most at home in a crowded café or in a public library, voices humming softly around them.

Recently, I was talking to my friend Don, telling him about *querencia*. He said, "Yes, *querer*—it means the wanting place." He helped me realize that for writers, that burning urge to write is our *querencia*. In order to feel at home we have to be writing. We feel awful if we haven't written in a week, if we don't write in our journals every day. Writing is a way of finding and keeping our home.

At home, in daylight, I retreat to my study to write, to gather strength, to fill up again. I feel most at home during the day, sitting in my writing chair with my feet up, a cup of coffee or tea on the desk. It's difficult for me to find my *querencia* and write at night.

When I don't have quiet in my life I sometimes ignore the pull toward that chair: it seems more important to make phone calls and pay bills. But I'm ignoring the voice that will lead me to safety, take me home. My body knows it. I feel cranky and life seems dull. The more I write, the more I have the urge to write, and the closer I come to finding my way home.

Write about where you feel most at home, where your querencia *is. Describe it in such clear detail that you feel you're there. Gather photographs and pictures of your* querencia *and tape them to your wall or carry them with you. Search for your* querencia. *Keep asking yourself: Where do I come from? Where do I feel most at home? Where do I feel most happy and relaxed? What is my ideal writing environment? Where can I write with my full powers?*

Poetry Inside Us All

IN THE small town of Ganado, Arizona, on the Navajo Nation, snow was ripe and crunchy under my boots, the sky wide and blue, the air so cold even my thick gloves couldn't warm my hands. I walked into the small elementary school to work with teachers and students for a week. Before meeting with students, I led a writers workshop for teachers. The cozy teachers room was unusual in that it had crowded bookcases, comfortable couches, and freshly made coffee. After we had introduced ourselves, I began talking about the importance of poetry and how even if we aren't conscious of it, there is poetry inside us all.

One man looked at me with a serious face and said, "There is no poetry inside of me." I looked back at him, a little startled, but I could see that others were relieved that he had spoken what was on their minds as well.

Most of these Navajo teachers had attended Bureau of Indian Affairs schools, sometimes hundreds of miles away from their homes. The U. S. government had set up the schools to deny the Navajos their culture and to propagate white culture. Speaking Navajo was forbidden and punishable—Navajo cultural ways were not learned or celebrated except on vacations, when the children went home to their families. Many of these teachers had read Shakespeare and Keats and had learned that writing was something for other people, certainly not for them.

I asked the man with the serious face what he taught his students about Navajo culture. "Well, a lot of different things," he said.

"Like what?" I persisted.

"Like, for instance, the Navajo names of the months."

"Can you give me an example?"

"For instance, what you call October is called Ghąąjí̜ in Navajo—the month of the dividing of the seasons. Ghąąjí̜ means back to back and refers to the fact that for six months the yellow of summer has been walking forward. Now the yellow of summer meets the white of winter. They turn their backs on each other. Summer walks back, and winter walks forward. It is the dividing of our season. It is the beginning of the Navajo new year."

A few of his colleagues who already considered them-selves poets said in unison, "That sounds like poetry to me."

He looked shocked. "That's poetry? I thought it had to rhyme."

After that first day, teachers stopped me in the hall in between my classes with their students to hand me poems they'd written. Jackie Chee gave me this poem about her regret for not having learned the Navajo ways from her grandmother:

The Song

I can hear her singing
to herself but also to me
Her songs are of everything
the rain, the mountains, the sun

She speaks in that gentle voice
Listen to these songs, she'awee

These are your songs now
For you to know is to live by what she says
I wish I knew then
that her words were true
Now I cannot sing the songs
of my grandmother
to my children

There are many times when I've felt that there was no poetry inside me, that I had nothing valuable to say. That the real writers were other people. It has taken me a while to believe that the way I feel each day, and the way I and others speak when we're least self-conscious, is where writing comes from. When we begin to speak in the language that is ours and tell our own stories and truths, we are surprised that this too is poetry.

Your own stories, thoughts, and language are the stuff of writing. Not, as many of you may feel, the sanitized versions of your selves and your lives. Maybe you feel you have nothing to say because you're excluding your own real, ordinary, and beautiful life. Does this sound like an accurate portrait of how you sometimes feel about yourself? Write down your thoughts about this. One of the first rules of writing is to try to write in your own voice. Write a brief description of something you did or saw today, and write it in a voice that is absolutely yours. Resist any attempt to transform it into Great Literature. Make the writing sound as much like you as possible.

Where Does Writing Hide?

Valentine for Ernest Mann
by Naomi Shihab Nye

You can't order a poem like you order a taco.
Walk up to the counter, say, "I'll take two"
and expect it to be handed back to you
on a shiny plate.

Still, I like your spirit.
Anyone who says, "Here's my address,
write me a poem," deserves something in reply.
So I'll tell you a secret instead:
poems hide. In the bottoms of our shoes,
they are sleeping. They are the shadows
drifting across our ceilings the moment
before we wake up. What we have to do
is live in a way that lets us find them.

Once I knew a man who gave his wife
two skunks for a valentine.

He couldn't understand why she was crying.
"I thought they had such beautiful eyes."
And he was serious. He was a serious man
who lived in a serious way. Nothing was ugly
just because the world said so. He really
liked those skunks. So, he re-invented them
as valentines and they became beautiful.
At least, to him. And the poems that had been
    hiding
in the eyes of skunks for centuries
crawled out and curled up at his feet.

Maybe if we re-invent whatever our lives give us
we find poems. Check your garage, the odd
    sock
in your drawer, the person you almost like, but
    not quite.
And let me know.

Many of us grew up thinking that ideas for writing come
from the fascinating and adventurous lives of writers. What
I love about this poem is that it dispels that myth and
reminds us that poems, and all writing, are hiding in the
most ordinary and familiar places—if we can only change
our way of looking at them.

At a recent workshop I asked people to list where poems
hide in their lives. Here are some of the places they named:
in my father's chair, in spider webs attached to the walls of
the garage, in the taste of spinach in my mouth, in my
mother's silence. Their catalogue itself sounded like a poem,
it was so vivid and surprising.

We don't necessarily have to change our lives around to
be writers or to be writing more. We must change the way

we look at our lives. By looking at the small, everyday circumstances and happenings, we find ideas to fill volumes.

Make a list of places where writing hides for you. Be specific. Instead of "Nature," say "In the oak leaves frozen in the pond." Instead of "Memories," write "In the papery skin of my grandmother's hands." Check around your life, and you'll find an abundance of writing ideas.

An Angel on My Shoulder

ONE SPRING I went on a long hike in the Sabino Canyon in Tucson. It was after rare torrential rains; the washes were rapids and had swept away many of the trail markers. I jumped on small islands of rock, waded through fast water, and searched the opposite bank for something that resembled a trail. Every once in a while I panicked as I watched the sun slide farther and farther behind the mountain. But then a voice would say, *Don't worry. You'll find your way back. It is not your fate to freeze tonight in this beautiful canyon.* This was the good angel who sometimes sits on my shoulder and talks to me in her soothing, assuring voice.

Sometimes writing feels like I'm lost in the canyon and will lose my way home. Writing is this serious. This much a test of my courage. This scary. Sometimes. But I must remember there is always a good angel on my shoulder guiding me back to the path. *Write what's in your heart,* she says. *Write the truth.*

Unfortunately, I also carry other voices around with me. When I write, those critical voices sometimes insult my soul. *Do you think you can write? What do you have to say anyway? Will your writing really be around in a hundred years? Where will you*

13

publish this one? How will you make a living? When I listen to these voices, I lose the trail that inspires me to write because I need and want to, because it gives me joy to speak, because it is vital to my existence. For women, these voices can be particularly censoring: You *feel* what? *Keep it to yourself,* they say. And women have kept silent for centuries.

Sometimes the inner critics' voices are insistent. Their goal is either to silence or to tame me, to dampen my courage and my risk taking, to keep me from telling the truth. Jimmy Santiago Baca has some good advice: "Write to the maddened drum of your own passions, and don't let your imagination be tamed by the sterile pronouncements of critics."

In order to write, you must face your inner critics, steal their power. Begin by trying to identify them. The more ambiguous they are, the more power they have. Write down: Who are they? What do they look like? Where do they work? At a university? At a magazine? How did they acquire so much power? When did they enter your life? In second grade, when your teacher threw your writing in the trash? In college, when your professor wrote huge X's all over the poems he didn't like? Last week, when you received four rejections in the mail? Describe them and what they're saying to you.

Write a letter telling them exactly how you feel about them, how you're going to protect yourself, what plans you have despite what they say. Whenever they speak to you, speak back. Get angry. It also helps to describe the fears you have of writing: is it the fear of failure? of feeling not smart enough? the fear that someone close to you will read what you wrote and feel hurt? It's important to expose these fears so you can clear them out and write freely.

For strength, listen to the good angel. The voice inside who knows and loves you. Write a letter to the good angel, the part of yourself that believes in what you're doing. Tell your hopes and dreams. How you want to be protected. What you would want someone very loving to tell you about your writing. What you need in order to be able to write. What you want to accomplish. Keep this letter beside you. Pin it to the wall near where you write. Go back to it. Reread it often. Keep the good angel on your shoulder. That voice will gain power as you begin to listen.

Feng Shui

As I walked into Cézanne's studio in Aix-en-Provence, I was struck immediately by how happy and creative it felt: huge floor-to-ceiling windows on the north side framing green-leafed trees, heavy drapes on either side; old tobacco tins; a pair of worn leather shoes; a cracked vase on a shelf; Cézanne's palette thick with dry paint. Outside, a bench nestled in the trees, and a path led through the garden to a spot overlooking Mont Sainte-Victoire, the mountain he was obsessed with and painted again and again.

The Chinese have a term for the feeling a place like Cézanne's studio exudes, a place steeped in creative energy and harmony: *feng shui*. The term comes from the Chinese characters for 'wind' and 'water'—both vital and powerful forces according to Chinese belief and important in determining whether someone's life is balanced and in harmony. There are *feng shui* experts in parts of Asia today who are well paid for their wisdom in determining if a building, a house, a grave, is situated in a proper place. Although the ancient practice of *feng shui* is complex, and I'm not an expert, I have intuitive feelings about places: when I enter a room or a house I can feel whether or not it's happy, whether the lives lived inside are in harmony.

Lin Yun, a *feng shui* expert, has said:

> We possess many senses, not just the five common senses—hearing, smelling, tasting, seeing, and touching—but many more. We all have insights. We pick up feelings from people, places, dreams, atmospheric energy. Some people give us a sense of foreboding. Some places make us feel happy and comfortable. We pick up these yet-to-be-named feelings and intuit reality and destiny from that. . . . If you are sensitive enough when you enter a house, you have various feelings—some give you a happy feeling, some make you uncomfortable and depressed.

Writers need to pay attention to these intuitive feelings. We need to make where we live, work, and write places with good *feng shui*. This has nothing to do with how expensive or how big they are: I've felt a sense of foreboding as soon as I've walked in the door of some grand houses, and I've walked into one-room apartments that feel happy and balanced. I can write anywhere as long as I have light, a place to put my feet up, and a cup of tea or coffee by my side—in a place that feels like it has some life in it, with no television set or fluorescent lights glaring. I try to make the place where I write as safe, soothing, and quiet as possible. A place where I can shut the door, have some solitude, and just be. For years I sat at a desk to write, and for years I felt uncomfortable. So I bought a writing chair that is big enough to nestle in. On the phone beside me I have taped this quotation: "Never get so busy making a living that you forget to make a life." I also collect remembrances from the places I've traveled to remind me of the vast beauty of this world, places from which I gather much of my inspiration:

a piece of dried wood sculpted by the New Mexico wind and sun, feathers left by Canadian geese in Texas, a red stone from the Arizona desert.

Feng shui is intertwined with the Chinese idea of *ch'i*, or 'life force.' *Ch'i* is what makes the geraniums on my windowsill bloom, it's the flow of water in rivers and streams; when someone is said to have a green thumb, they are a good tender of *ch'i*. *Ch'i* is similar to the Christian idea of the soul. But *ch'i* can also be blocked or weak. Sometimes I meet someone and feel uncomfortable around him but don't know why, or a restaurant feels claustrophobic and I know I can't write there—all this has to do with *ch'i*, that life force, being blocked.

I have to surround myself with what will give me courage and affirm the work I'm doing, a physical space that is mine where I can write.

Try to identify places you've lived or visited that have good feng shui. *Describe them—why do they feel like they're in harmony? When you're trying to find a place to write, use your intuition to figure out what this place might hold. What are your criteria for balance and harmony? Where do you like to write? Do you have a corner, a couch, or a chair in your house that feels like a good place to write? Do you need to have quiet, voices, music, a lot of excitement around you?*

Wherever your writing place is, make it a place that awaits you with open and loving arms. Don't be afraid to take up a little room in the world to give yourself the freedom to write.

Doing What I Have To

I WROTE my first book in nightly two-hour increments after driving around 113th and 114th Streets for an hour looking for a parking place. I would sit on the couch in my closet apartment, sirens and car alarms blaring outside my window. I finished it in nine months. I did what I had to in order to write.

Try as we must to make a place for ourselves that nurtures our writing, we have to tolerate a lot of imperfection: messy houses, noise, rejection, no one's believing in what we're doing, early morning or late night hours, writer's block. I do all I can to clear out my life, but in the end there are obligations, distractions, and messes, and I write anyway.

While writing this book I didn't vacuum my house for four months. The spiders were ecstatic. They wove their sticky webs over everything, connecting chair to couch to table. Each time I passed I would look the other way, pretending not to notice that they had moved in, this time for good. Dust balls roamed freely. I temporarily lost some of my friends. They began to leave messages on my answering machine: "I hope you're okay. I haven't heard from you in months. Call me back." I was obsessed.

Robert Bly says:

> To live sincerely is to live your own life, not your father's life or your mother's life or your neighbor's life; to spend soul on large concerns, not to waste your life as a kind of human ant carrying around small burdens; and finally, to live sincerely is to "live deep and suck out all the marrow of life," as Thoreau declares in *Walden*. That may require unsociability. Thoreau noticed that at a certain age boys remain in shadows and corners of rooms, look a little wild, make up their minds about a given grownup in a second, and may come to supper or not. Thoreau values that unsociability in both boys and girls. But those moments soon disappear, replaced by an old anxiety to please.

These words are pinned on my wall, and despite their gender stereotype, they are useful to me as I'm immersed in this book and I feel the guilt of all the things not done. And in the end, I'll vacuum my house and invite friends for dinner. But I'll also have made an important decision— momentarily to give my heart and time over to my writing as much as I can, to give myself the freedom to create, and to value that creation over all the nagging chores that need to get done.

Make a list of some of the chores and obligations that are nagging you. Look at each one carefully: which ones are absolutely essential? which ones can wait a day or two—a week—even a month? Try to attend to your obligations when you're tired; save your best energy for writing.

Time-Worlds

MANY INDIGENOUS cultures have no word for time. Their sense of time is not measured by clocks but by the earth: seasons and moons, births and deaths, sowing and harvesting. It wasn't until there were railroads that people began measuring time with watches in arbitrary intervals, then synchronized it all over the world.

Our culture is obsessed with time—particularly with not having enough. Writing needs a lot of time—not just the time it takes to put the words down on the page, but time to reflect, to ponder an idea, to read, to stare out a window, to go for a walk, to gather courage and strength. All of this requires immeasurable amounts of time. When people ask me how long it took to write my first book I say, "It took four years to think about it and another year to write."

My friend Marie and I talk on the phone a lot about how we never have enough time to write. We encourage each other to say no to more commitments that we would love to make but that would eat into our time for writing. She said to me one day, "For one line of poetry I write, it takes eight hours of seemingly doing nothing: sitting on my couch drinking coffee, staring out the window, taking a walk." It's true. Writing demands the illusion of infinite time: to stare, to sit at a café and write in a notebook.

Robert Grudin, author of *The Grace of Great Things*, writes about the importance of time:

> Creative people move purposefully across this continent of time, truly exploring it. The rest of us shack up in little patches and clearings of time, always harried, always distracted, slave to the next knock on the office door or phone call. Our professional lives show an alarmingly high percentage of "response activities"—meeting deadlines, obeying directives. . . . Creativity demands the opposite.

Writers carve out regularly scheduled periods of time. Grudin calls these expanses time-worlds.

But how do I do find more time within my hectic life? How is linked to why. If I know it's a matter of my survival to write, I will carve out this time. Half an hour before work, at lunch, after work, is enough time to write approximately three pages in my journal. If I carve this time out every day, writing becomes like eating or taking a shower or brushing my teeth. Things I must do every day become routine. I don't have to think about making time for them anymore, I just do them. Once I've made the time for writing, I can be free to think about my ideas and not about how I'm ever going to find the time to write them down.

Make a deep commitment to finding some time for writing in your life. Vow that you'll write every day in your notebook, at your typewriter, or on your computer. If you commute to work, get a magnetized pad

of paper and pen and stick them to the dashboard of your car; when a line or a thought occurs to you, write it down. Carry your notebook at all times. Carry a tape recorder and speak your thoughts into it as you're driving or taking the train. Make sure you write something every day. Once you get used to it, you'll begin to feel dissatisfied if you haven't.

Keeping the Channel Open

WHEN I was a girl, although no one in my family was religious, I prayed every night. I remember folding my hands and waiting for what I then called god to arrive. Inside my mind I saw a stage—a curtain behind my eyes—and the curtain opened and the presence of something that I remember as a deep, velvety black would appear and I would feel comforted. I spoke to this presence about my worries, my hopes, my fears, and my dreams. It was at these moments that I felt my heart opened. I could speak freely: I asked that everyone I loved would be taken care of, that I would do well in school. That presence was the essence of what gives me the freedom to speak now.

Taped on my current notebook are the words of Martha Graham to Agnes de Mille:

> There is a vitality, a life force, an energy, a quickening that is translated through you into action. And because there is only one of you in all time, this expression is unique and if you block it, it will never exist through any other medium, and be lost. The world will not have it.

It is not your business . . . to determine how good it is, nor how valuable, nor how it compares with other expressions. It is your business to keep the channel open. You do not even have to believe in yourself or your work. You have to keep open and aware directly to the urges that motivate you. Keep the channel open.

I know the times in my life when I've kept the channel open. For me it's often in the summer, when the day's light seems endless, when I swim each day, when dinners out on the porch with friends last for hours, when I devote the entire day to writing or sometimes painting.

There are hundreds of strategies artists have used in the past to keep from crawling into the narrow tunnel of tasks and obligations. Here are a few:

Go for a long walk
Meditate
Get a massage
Read Adrienne Rich, Gwendolyn Brooks, Emily Dickinson
Visit a café regularly and write in your journal there
Take a belly-dancing class
Read a biography of someone whose life you admire or despise
Plant bulbs
Hang a birdfeeder out your window and learn the names of birds
Take a bath with lit candles all around the edge of the tub
Organize a writers group
Attend a poetry reading
Visit a museum

Listen to music that will make you cry or dance
Sing—loudly and unashamedly
Make love
Run
Swim

Whatever activity you pursue, you know you're on the right track
when you feel that deep, velvety blackness, that comfort, that presence
that nourishes possibilities and words.

A Conversation with Myself

WRITING IS an act of faith: faith that what I have to say, how I see the world, are important. I listen. I see. I feel and I record. Keeping the words flowing is an act of faith.

Painters have brushes, paints, a palette, an easel—writers have notebooks. A notebook is an ear, always tuned in, always ready to hear more.

The act of writing feeds me. A notebook is a gathering place, a portfolio of thoughts and fragments that lead me to bigger projects. What I write, I write on impulse. What moves me to write one thing and not another is the point. My notebook is my filter of what's important and what's not.

Lining the shelf of the closet in my study are notebooks collected over ten years: red-spined Chinese notebooks with ivory lined paper, blue and brown spiral notebooks, small black sketchbooks, black-and-white-speckled composition books—all now marked and dated. They are a record of my life and hold seeds of future poems and books. I pull one of the Chinese notebooks off the shelf and open to a page:

> **March 28** Broadway Diner—6:00. Waiting for the traffic to thin although the drive will probably be hell no

matter what time it is. Stitches [from a wisdom-tooth extraction] taken out today. Tomorrow—one day off. Then two days' work. Then a week's vacation. I feel so utterly bone tired. I need to rest and write!

I remember this time. Desperate to find a few moments of breathing space and yearning for more.

April 1   Snowing in Sag Harbor. I can see the clock of the high school and the pine trees heavy with snow. Snow on the red blossoms of the tree next door. Snow on the budding daffodils and tulip leaves. Snow on the lilac bush not yet ready to blossom.

My voice has changed here, after one day off to write. An image that stays with me still. A seed of a poem perhaps?

April 2   Eavan Boland: "Now I wonder how many young women poets taught themselves in rooms like that, with a blank discipline—to write the poem that was in the air, rather than the one within their experience? How many faltered, as I did, not for lack of answers, but for lack of questions. *It will be a long time still, I think,* wrote Virginia Woolf, *before a woman can sit down to write a book without finding a phantom to be slain or a rock to be dashed.*"

I wrote from the air for a long time—not trusting that my experiences were worthy of writing. This is a good quotation to copy and tack to the wall near my writing chair.

April 13   Ironic Names—
In a Garden City industrial lot—a grey building called The Blue Sky Diner

My notebook is a constant weight in my already-too-heavy black bag as I try to find a few minutes to write over

28

scrambled eggs and coffee at a Queens diner or in the cramped seat of a plane heading to Arizona. Its presence always reminds me I'm a writer, and it helps me live a considered life that doesn't spin by focused only on groceries, dinner, and car repairs.

A notebook is a fertilizer for my writing, not just a record of daily events. It's a place to dream, to explore, to play. It's a companion. I try to tell the truth in my notebook—although as I read over some of the pages now I realize that I haven't been entirely truthful. I didn't always write about what I was really thinking at the time. Even in my notebook I censor. But I try to tell the truth to myself first and foremost.

Joan Didion writes: "So the point of my keeping a notebook has never been, nor is it now, to have an accurate factual record of what I have been doing or thinking. . . . *How it felt to me:* that is getting closer to the truth about a notebook."

Julia Cameron, in *The Artist's Way*, advises all artists to write what she calls morning pages: three pages in a notebook each morning, no matter what, without stopping, without judging, without rereading. Every day. Just write. Allow the mind to wonder. When I began writing morning pages it sometimes felt excruciating. I'd write the date at the top of the page, and then have nothing to say. But because of my month-long commitment to these morning pages, I began to learn to speak even when I wanted so desperately to be silent.

If you don't already keep a journal, buy a notebook. Choose one that will help make you feel it's inviting you to write down your own

words, in your own voice. Will a fancy, expensive notebook make your words seem too precious? Will a spiral notebook make you feel your words are important enough? Is your notebook too heavy or too big to carry around with you? Once you choose, leave the cover blank or decorate it with quotes, photos, or poems. This will be your companion.

Now, write in it. A notebook is a conversation with yourself. And it's your job as a writer to keep up the conversation.

I'm Not in the Military

IT TOOK me years to realize that as a writer I'm allergic to strict discipline. I have some writer friends who rise at six in the morning and write until evening without stopping even to think about lunch. To them, this doesn't feel like punishment. To me, it feels like I've joined the military. For years, I thought I could only be a real writer if I worked this way too. I rose in the morning only to get frustrated, tired, and hungry by ten o'clock. Then I got it: I don't like to work that way.

Now I have my own ritual: I walk. When I'm in New York I begin at Seventy-first Street and walk through Central Park to Strawberry Fields, the small park that Yoko Ono built as a memorial to John Lennon, over the mandala star with the word IMAGINE in large letters, then northward toward the lake past Bow Bridge, where boaters row and ducks swim in summer, past large shining outcroppings of the Manhattan schist that holds up the skyscrapers in midtown, to the wide playing field where Dobermans run and school children play soccer by the side of the Dragonfly Preserve, past a small grassy field where craggy fruit trees hold snow on their branches in winter and offer spectacular blossoms in spring, toward the Metropolitan Museum, and then turn my steps home again. The walk takes me about an hour. In winter, I'm bundled in hat, gloves, and scarf; by the time I arrive home I'm so warm I've unbuttoned my coat.

As I walk, I write. Words circle my head. I speak lines out loud to see how they'll sound. The rhythm of walking orders my mind and limbers me up for the hours I will sit in one place. When I finally do sit down to write, I've already been at it for an hour.

I've discovered that I'm more of the behavior modification kind of writer. When I write I always need a reward, like a cup of something hot next to me during the cold months or a cold drink during summer. I can work for hours at a time only if I know that down the lonely path is a piece of chocolate cake, a good movie, a hot bath, dinner with friends. If I can get a treat afterward, then I'll do my work. It took me a long time to listen to what I needed as a writer.

Find out what you need for writing that will make it easier for you to go on this journey. Test it out. Try sitting or lying down. Write first thing in the morning, then late at night. In a café, at home. Most of this will be dictated by the urgency of what you need to do. Pay attention to your needs and cultivate them. Try to find a ritual that will help you write. Maybe it will just be a shower in the morning and a cup of coffee. Or maybe you'll find that you must read the newspaper first. Or your favorite book. Or meditate. Whatever it is, search out the ways that will make writing easier for you.

The Rumble Beneath My Feet

I ONCE flew to Lawton, Oklahoma, to speak to English teachers at a conference. The morning of my speech I went down early to the dining room to eat breakfast; as I was taking a bite of poached egg and toast, the table and the water glasses began to shake and the floor rumbled beneath my feet.

I eyed the other people eating breakfast to see if they were as startled as I was—but no one looked up. I shrugged it off, but every ten minutes it kept happening. When the waitress gave me my check I asked, "Did you notice anything rumbling?"

"Oh, that," she said. "That's the artillery at Fort Sill."

When my conference host greeted me, I asked her about the rumble. She said, "Lawton is home to one of the largest artillery sites in the United States, Fort Sill. You get used to it after a while. In fact, during the Gulf War a lot of the guys were away, so it was silent around here. People would look around and say something was strange and then realize that they didn't hear any guns going off." Throughout my speech that morning, artillery exploded. The ground shook. And the faces of people in the audience didn't change.

During the flight home, I couldn't stop thinking about the rumble. Why had this disturbed me so much? I kept thinking about the lives of people in Lawton: people sitting down for breakfast to the sound of missiles being fired, in the shower as shells exploded underground, children in the elementary school singing above the noise of guns, lying on their mats during rest time lulled to sleep by the firing of artillery, the rumbles a constant reminder of the military and its job of destruction.

I wondered if I could write anything while guns were being fired around me. Sometimes, losing our voices is a natural outcome of trying to ignore what bothers us.

What are the rumbles in your everyday life? Are there things that happen to you each day that are too painful to notice? that you feel resigned and helpless about so you have stopped paying attention? that keep you from writing? Does someone close to you undermine you? Is a job or a relationship sapping your energy? A lot of people who grew up in homes filled with daily rumbling tend to re-create the same situations. It's important to try to clear the air and tell the truth. Writing can help you pay attention to your life. Write about what bothers you. What's rumbling for you? After you write, ask yourself: What prevents me from seeing or changing my situation?

Sometimes it takes a while to clear away the rumbling, to create the environment you need—but it's still important to write. You don't need perfect conditions, but you do need to be honest and pay attention. Write your way into clarity.

The Education of the Eye:
Staring

WALKER EVANS once hid a camera in his jacket and photographed people in the Manhattan subway. The photographs show faces in quiet repose: a woman with a black hat, her mouth pursed disapprovingly toward the camera, a big-cheeked child's eyes turned in the same direction; a profile of a woman with a big black hat and pencil-thin eyebrows; a blind man walking down the aisle playing the accordion; people staring indifferently ahead, as they do now at people asking for money. Evans' camera is our eye as he catches glimpses of people on the way home from work, after shopping, after a day with relatives. He once advised: "Stare. Educate your eye. Die knowing something. You are not here long."

Sometimes I try to look at the world through a lens that reveals unexpected beauty: I see an old man on the street, ravaged and shuffling along Broadway with a cane, his face fierce and determined; or a little girl, dressed in black patent leather shoes, a black velvet cape, and white gloves, walking happily down the street, holding hands with her mother. I used to feel too polite and awkward to look. I was taught that staring is rude. But so much goes by unseen if we always avert our gaze. The street can educate our eyes and mind, if we let it.

When I was a teenager my best friend and I used to drive to National Airport on Friday nights to watch people. We sat in chairs and watched as people walked quickly by, greeted one another, yawned, ate, or waited for a plane. We would tell each other little narratives: that one's sure in a hurry, that one doesn't spend enough time with his kids, that one has dark circles under her eyes. We would notice gold buckles on shoes, the hurried rhythm of people's steps as they walked to their gate, who was there to greet them, whether or not they dyed their hair; we tried to notice everything. I didn't know it then, but we were writing. We were capturing a little bit of the world. If I had had a notebook, I could have captured it more permanently.

I remember when I learned to see colors. A friend and I were driving slowly along the streets of Washington, caught in traffic because there was construction ahead. I was getting more and more impatient. "Look what they're do-ing," I said to my friend, who was a painter. "It's so ugly, the earth torn up like that." And it was true; in one sense it was ugly. But he said, "Look how beautiful it is. Look at that yellow crane against that green fence. And have you ever seen anything as blue as that?" I turned my head to look and a world of colors opened. As we sat in the stifling heat, I waded in the colors at the construction site. He had edu-cated my eye, and I saw the world differently.

Since then I have educated my eye to see other things as well; I look at the world through the clarifying and sometimes painful lens of justice. One day I was sitting in a restaurant and watched a man on the street ask for some change from every person who passed by. I was amazed that after an hour of his repeating "Please, can you spare some change?" over and over, only a few people out of hundreds acknowledged that he was there by looking him in the face to say, "No, I'm sorry, I can't," and only one person gave him money. Everyone else pretended he wasn't there. I thought about how many times I had done the very same thing, and I could see how inhumane and crazy-making that is for the poor on the streets. Staring invites me into people's lives, opens my heart, lets me feel what I see.

Go to a public place: a coffee shop, an airport, a neighborhood grocery store, the subway. Bring your notebook. Think of it as a camera. Be a word photographer of people: their shoes, hair, smells, what they eat, how they speak. Record it. Make up stories about the people you see. Invent their lives from the details you have absorbed: where they live and work, who lives with them, their history. Try to notice everything. Pay special attention to people you would ordinarily never notice, who live invisible lives. Grace Paley urges writers to "go in and out of ivory / towers and two-room apartments on Avenue C / and buckwheat fields and army camps." Pour your observations into words.

Don't Try to Avoid the Rocks

MARIE TOLD me this story: She went to teach a poetry workshop in Taos, New Mexico, and afterward took a rafting trip down the Rio Grande. The river guides explained to her group some of the dangers of rafting this particular section during July, when the water was so low. The guide kept stressing one rule above all others: *Don't try to avoid the rocks. Let your raft bump into them. The rocks will help you maneuver around the difficult places so you can proceed smoothly down the river.*

Marie said that when they spotted a rock, their first instinct was to try to steer clear. But whenever they tried, they would get stuck. Eventually, people got it. They saw a rock, bumped into it, bounced off, and glided backward. The current did the rest.

I now have this crucial metaphor written out and pinned near my writing chair: DON'T TRY TO AVOID THE ROCKS. The obstacles I face—lack of time, too many projects at once—as well as the obstacles all writers face—rejection, criticism, doubts and insecurities, unfinished poems and stories—are impossible to avoid and can be valuable teachers. I can gather strength from them. They are inevitable parts of a writer's life.

What are the rocks in the currents of your writing life? What obstacles keep you from writing? Becoming aware of what is blocking you sometimes leads to a solution.

Let Writing Lead the Way

TWO YEARS ago I began writing a memoir, a series of recurring images from childhood. Here is one of them:

Flag

Early evening on the porch, my hand over my heart as a bugle played Taps. I looked up, pulled the ropes, and the flag lowered. Then, careful not to let the corner touch the ground, my sister and I folded it into triangles and placed it in its box.

What a promise it was, folded up at night. It was a snake in my heart. It was a secret coiled, the spring broken. *Do not let it touch the ground. Do not let even one corner of it touch the ground. Do not let it touch the ground. Otherwise, we'll have to burn it. We'll have to burn the flag.*

After fifty or so pages I decided that no reader would be able to understand these fragmented memories. So I changed my approach, imposed a more traditional chronological narrative structure. For months I worked and worked. Finally I stopped and looked at what I had done. It was terrible. The language that had begun as poetic and metaphoric had lost all its life. The book was doomed. Thinking about what had happened, I realized that I had not listened to what the book wanted. I had changed the intent of the writing, just as people move a stream by redirecting its banks, hoping the water will obey. It never does. Neither did my writing.

And so, after a period of silence, I went back to where I had been months before and began again and am still working, letting the writing do what it wants.

An artist, whose name I wish I hadn't forgotten, said, "A work of art uses the artist to get itself done; as I work I am able to find out what it wants to be." When I'm writing I know what this feels like. It's being receptive, trusting that the writing will tell me what it needs.

Reread what you've written. Listen to what it's telling you. What does it want to be? a poem? a story? a memoir? an essay? What other images and thoughts occur to you? It might seem frightening to allow the writing to guide you but try to relax, and don't panic if it wants to take you into strange and uncharted water.

The Intent, Not the Recipe

ON A cold winter morning two friends and I walk down the street to Shopsin's restaurant in Greenwich Village. Shopsin's is decidedly funky—car seats as booths, creaky wooden floors, the air thick with grill smoke and the smell of bacon. It doesn't feel like a restaurant in the heart of Greenwich Village, but like a sleepy Vermont diner that's been around as long as anyone in town can remember. The decor is idiosyncratic and homey. Plastic lizards sit on the window-sill, oil paintings of Mr. and Mrs. Shopsin line the walls, at our table we roll an eight ball back and forth. Mr. Shopsin, aproned chef and co-owner (with his wife), sits at one of the booths, a headband tied around his grey bushy hair, while his young son, out of school for the December holi-day, takes our order.

The best part of Shopsin's is the food. The menu is staggering. The breakfast menu is five pages long. The lunch and dinner menu fills six pages, the first of which is devoted to soups, over one hundred of them, with exotic and poetic names like Senegalese Cherry, Eggplant Jerk, Plantain Co-riander, Sweet Potato Jalapeño, Pear Prosciutto, African Green Curry, Florida Peanut, Pistachio Turkey Verde, and

42

Turkey Slumgullion. Reading the names out loud makes our mouths water.

"How is it possible to offer over one hundred soups plus all the other five pages of the menu in a place so small?" I ask Mr. Shopsin.

"It's all about changing the way you look at things," he says. "You look at something and think you see it one way— but if you just change the way you look at it, it becomes something else. From five basic stocks I can make an infinite variety of soups. Because after all, what's important is the intent, not the recipe."

That's true in writing: following a recipe never works. Words become brittle, won't pour into the mold we try so hard to fit them into. That's why writing from an outline usually produces something flat and formulaic.

From the twenty-six letters in the alphabet, writers create an infinite variety of writing but not by following a recipe. We all begin with the basics, but then we improvise. One pinch of coriander and a few plantains will change a basic stock into Plantain Coriander. We writers have to feel our way like chefs—lifting spoonfuls to our mouths to taste, adding more salt and spices, intuiting when the soup is done.

What are the topics, words, and phrases that are distinctively yours? Write as if you're talking to your best friend: in your own voice and with words that you would actually speak. You can write about anything—even subjects that have been worn into clichés, like the stars or a sunset—as long as you write about it in your own inimitable voice.

Digging Beneath the Surface

BEFORE I moved to New York my head was filled with stereotypes. Friends would say, "New York! It's so dirty. It smells. It's dangerous. Don't ever get lost above 125th Street." New York was a fearful place—the quintessence of urban horror.

When I began to teach writing in the schools, I traveled to neighborhoods all over the city and learned that places where many people were afraid to go had been distorted by a kind of racism fueled by newspaper and TV reports. As I rode the subway or drove to the Bronx, to Brooklyn, to Washington Heights, to Far Rockaway, I began to see for myself what the city was really like. In the Bronx I saw the reality behind what seems a wasteland to people from out of town who pass at sixty miles an hour on the Cross Bronx Expressway: it is home to hundreds of children and a working neighborhood to their families. New York changed from an abstract place of possible danger to a city of a multitude of cultures and peoples in distinct neighborhoods.

My friend Steve, who grew up in New York, also helped me know the city. We frequently took walks to Harlem—his old neighborhood. We walked to Antzis' Live Poultry Shop at 126th Street and Amsterdam Avenue. Inside, in stacked silver cages, were chickens, quails, ducks, guinea hens, pheasants, rabbits, even pigeons, crowded one on top another; on Saturdays it bustles with people buying fowl for big Sunday dinners. From Antzis' we walked past stores selling cuchifritos and sat at a table at M & G Soul Food and ate fried chicken. It was like a small town: everyone knew everyone else. We walked to La Marqueta on Park Avenue and 116th Street near Luis Munoz Marin Boulevard; we walked by El Pez de Oro, where Sal, Jerry, and Mike sell fresh fish and chicken and Rosa sells fabrics, where you can find a good cup of coffee or a whole fish. On the way home, we passed vacant lots, saw people sitting on car seats, listened to them chatting on the sidewalk, heard their radios blaring. Abstract New York City came alive.

Rilke wrote:

> For the sake of a single poem, you must see many cities, many people and things, you must understand animals, must feel how birds fly, and know the gestures which small flowers make when they open in the morning. You must be able to think back to streets in unknown neighborhoods, to unexpected encounters, and to partings you had long seen coming.

And Audre Lorde advises:

> For those of us who write, it is necessary to scrutinize not only the truth of what we speak, but the truth of that language by which we speak it.

The task of every writer is to dig beneath the surface and find complexity in each situation. A writer can't afford to be lazy. The work of a writer is to refuse to accept stereotypes, to see for herself what's really true. It's too easy to go with the abstract, not to be grounded in the concrete, the examined, the specific. This insistence on the deeper layers of knowing is a way of life.

Begin with your neighborhood. Beyond what anyone's told you, what do you really see? Do a little research: find out its history. Look into people's faces, watch their gestures to find out what they're not saying. Challenge any stereotype about people, neighborhoods, cities that you hear. Accept no one's vision but your own. Examine the stereotypes in your writing. Is the word dark *always applied to anything negative or bad? There's a stereotype you need to challenge.*

Incarnadine Seas

Precipice. Fleece. Nettle. Spalling. Paucity. Pallid. Bleating. Thirsty.
Words collected like shiny red tomatoes picked from the vine, ripening in my word notebook. When I read a word I like in the newspaper or a book or if I overhear one, I write it down. I collect words for their music, their poetry, their possibilities, their surprises. I haunt used-book stores, searching for books that contain unusual words. *Elementary Seamanship* has a glossary of sea terms. *scupper, bulwark, winch, windlass, scuttles.* The book is a cup of possibility for those days when I'm thirsty for words.

In a bookstore in Vermont I found an old English primer, published in the early 1900s, whose exercises are like poetry:

> The Pupil may now describe the analogy between the following words:
>
> 1. The wings of a bird and the legs of an animal.
>
> 2. Snow and rain.
>
> 3. Genius and the sun.
>
> 4. A watch and an animal.

In a class at Columbia University, Derek Walcott waxed passionately about Shakespeare's "incarnadine seas," saying that these two words were exquisite together. He wrote the words on the board and made us say them, hoping that he could teach us to swoon over language too. I had never before heard anyone love words so deeply.

Gwendolyn Brooks says, "COLLECT WORDS! Buy your own dictionary. Read your dictionary every day. CIRCLE exciting words. The more words you know, the better you will be able to express yourself, your thoughts."

To be a writer, it's necessary to have a passionate love affair with words. To say words we love is like kissing; we can feel the pleasure all over our body.

Pablo Neruda writes,

It's the words that sing, they soar and descend . . . I bow to them . . . I love them, I cling to them, I run them down, I bite into them, I melt them down . . . I love words so much . . . The unexpected ones . . . The ones I wait for greedily or stalk until, suddenly, they drop . . . Vowels I love . . . They glitter like colored stones, they leap like silver fish, they are foam, thread, metal, dew . . . I run after certain words . . . They are so beautiful that I want to fit them all into my poem . . . I catch them in mid-flight, as they buzz past, I trap them, clean them, peel them, I set myself in front of the dish, they have a crystalline texture to me, vibrant, ivory, vegetable, oily, like fruit, like algae, like agates, like olives . . . And then I stir them, I shake them, I drink them, I gulp them down, I mash them, I garnish them, I let them go . . . I leave them in my poem like stalactites, like slivers of polished wood, like coals, pickings from a shipwreck, gifts from the waves . . . Everything exists in the word.

I collect words because I love them, and as a writer I need to be able to pepper my writing with words from everywhere.

In your notebook, include a place for words you love. Listen to words spoken around you, write down words from menus, signs, books, newspapers—the more you become aware of the words possible to you, the more abundant your writing will become.

Everything, Including the Kitchen Sink

IN THE dark, stained-glass-windowed cafeteria at Teachers College a woman was transforming her life. One of my older graduate students was going through a difficult divorce, and I knew it. Yet each week she brought in poems that were polite and nice. When she talked, I could hear her rage. One day I said to her, "Just talk to me. Tell me what's going on with you." I wrote down what she said. At first she was vague, but then she began to use words that were ordinary, jagged, everyday words. When she spoke she situated herself at the kitchen sink, when she first found out that her husband was having an affair, how she looked long and hard at the sponge and the Comet as if to take her eyes away from them would be to lose everything she had. When she finished, I said, "Do you know how different your language is when you talk? It's so different from how you write." She said, "I could never use those words in my writing, though, because . . . because . . . they're so unpoetic. They're so common."

And then it became clear. Her version of writing was like a woman's in the 1700s—a woman oppressed even in her speech. She was supposed to be a nice girl even when what was raging inside didn't fit the image. I asked her to read Sharon Olds and Adrienne Rich. I asked her to read Maxine Kumin's "Excrement."

I asked her to list in her journal all the words she thought she wasn't supposed to use in her writing. The so-called common words. The next week she came back with her list: *trash can, sponge, disposal, toenail, divorce.* Her next assignment was to try to write using as many "unpoetic" words as she could. The more unpoetic the better. Her poetry was transformed. By using words that she spoke every day, her images became less abstract and distanced and more expressive of how she really felt.

We writers can't be afraid to get our hands dirty. We need to dig in the mud, put our fingers down clogged drains, get dirt under our fingernails. We have to be able to muck around, and our language has to reflect the "common." It's impossible to tell the truth about our lives otherwise.

Make a list of the most "unpoetic" words you can think of: common words that you perceive as too far below the realm of Literature. Make a point of including these words in your writing. Using this everyday language will help you make your writing more specific.

I Could Not Tell

HIDDEN AWAY in the wordless places of my heart are my deepest secrets, wrapped in silence and sometimes shame. These are the subjects that I don't write about easily, and I have a hundred excuses for avoiding them: I don't want to hurt anyone's feelings, I don't want people to think I'm a weirdo, they make me feel like a bad person. Well, here's some news: all people have secrets, and all writers are weirdos. Knowing this full well, Muriel Rukeyser asked her students to begin there, by writing "I could not tell . . ." at the top of the page. She knew that what's hidden away, stored up, in all of us is our most honest, electric, and true power.

When I wrote my list of "I could not tells," I first spewed out a few decoys: I used to scare my sister with a straw doll, I first made love under the Washington Monument. But beyond these relatively harmless pseudosecrets are the real ones. When I even think them, I look over my shoulder to see whether anyone is looking. These are more difficult to write about and need a fortress of safety before I can reveal them; they are not included in the catalogue that I would read to a strange audience of a hundred. For these secrets I must set up a safety mechanism: I can write them down, but

I must quickly burn them or scribble over them with black Magic Marker.

The truth is that none of our secrets are ever as bad as we think. When I've revealed some of mine to my best friends, they've practically yawned at the ordinariness of my confessions. In my silence there is a lot of locked power that I could use in my writing. Michelle Cliff writes, "I hid from my real sources. But my real sources were also hidden from me." The first step is to learn to write from my real sources. If I hide who I am from the world, I can get so used to it that I begin to hide from myself as well.

Write "I could not tell . . ." on the top of the page, and begin your list. Put down a few fake secrets first, if you must, but then dig in and reveal what you didn't before. Feel the power your secrets unleash.

Writing Is Like Making Tortillas

SOME OF my students in Arizona have taught me that writing is very much like making tortillas. When you make a tortilla, you pinch a small amount of dough in your fingers first, then work it carefully in your damp hands, slapping, clapping, and turning it from palm to palm, right hand to left. This is where the art comes in; you must be careful not to puncture it with your fingers but still be vigorous enough to continue flattening and thinning it. You can't force it or lose confidence, because it will either tear or be lumpy and uneven. I was told that in the early mornings, in some small villages in Mexico, you once could hear the light clapping noises until all the *masa* had been molded into thin translucent spheres, ready to be cooked.

Making tortillas is an artful technique, and a new practitioner produces hundreds and hundreds of uneven, hole-ridden tortillas before she gets them to look round and thin. But when you watch people who have made thousands of them, it looks graceful and easy. The magic in the art of making tortillas—and in the art of writing—is revealed in this old saying: "What is it that goes along the foothills of the mountains patting out tortillas with its hands? A butterfly?"

On some rare days writing feels like this, easy and smooth as a butterfly, but most of the time it feels like hard work: I leave holes in my writing, it's uneven, it torments me. It's important to remember that some days the work will seem easy but that I will also produce many tortillas full of holes.

Try making corn tortillas. Here's a recipe:

> 2 *cups masa farina*
> 1-1/4 *cups warm water*

In a bowl combine the flour and water. Using your bare hands, knead the dough well until it is completely smooth. Moisten your hands with water and take a small piece of dough and roll it into a one-inch ball. Press it out between your palms, extending it with small pats, first on one palm and then the other, turning your hands over as you do so. It takes about thirty-three pats to make a tortilla five inches round.

> *Heat an ungreased comal or griddle. Lay the tortilla flat on the comal. Leave for five seconds, flip, cook the other side for thirty seconds, then flip back to the first side for fifteen seconds.*

> *Place tortillas one on top of the other in a basket, and cover with a cloth to keep in heat and preserve freshness.*

Picking Up a Stone

SOMETIMES ON my walks at Sagaponack Beach I search for stones to carry with me. Stones carried by the sea, held for centuries and cast out on the shore. I pick one up—it is radiantly orange, shiny, salty, and round. I put it in my jacket pocket. My fingers reach for it, roll it around, feel a rough spot, a dent, notice how the sea polished it smooth. I begin to know it. I take it out and look at it again; now that it's dry, I see that what I first thought was orange is really multicolored, mixed with swirls of white and red. I return the stone to my pocket and my hand holds it tight as I walk, this time feeling how light it is. I bring it home, place it on the windowsill. As I'm writing, I glance at it again, the light pale outside, and I notice something new. And so the stone I picked up by the ocean becomes familiar on my windowsill, and I know its shape, its colors, its textures more intimately.

Writing is often like picking up of a stone on the beach. Contrary to what I was taught in school, writing isn't a scientific formula: think of topic, make outline, write topic sentence, write introductory paragraph, then write the rest.

Before I write one word there is a world of thinking, reflecting, and imagining that takes place, sometimes without my even being aware of it.

Imagine something you want to write about is a stone you've picked up on the beach. Roll the image, the idea, the thought, or the feeling around in your mind. This gestation period is an important part of writing. If you give your thoughts a chance to gather weight and depth, when you do finally sit down to write, the life of the work will have already begun.

Digging in the Earth

MY HANDS dig deep into the dirt already loosened by the shovel. I'm preparing the earth for new vegetable seeds and flowers, and my fingers work the soil over and over. Spots that haven't been turned for years are dark and wet from having been buried for so long. My bare hands suddenly encounter small, jumping wormlike insects. When exposed to the light for the first time they pop as if in pain. These mystery insects have probably never before seen light in their brief lives, and they struggle like fish out of water. I quickly bury them again.

When I'm writing and I have a sudden and painful realization about my life, my insides behave like these beautiful struggling creatures, wriggle like worms in the light. I let writing like this incubate in my notebook until I'm ready to transform it—which may be never. I seldom turn that raw painful recollection or feeling into a poem or a piece of writing immediately; time needs to go by, the pain to fade. Galway Kinnell says that this kind of writing is wet like a newborn and needs to be treated as such. It took me a long time to know this. I thought that my writing would be better if I forced every painful feeling into a poem quickly. Telling the truth about my life is important—but true writing takes time and patience until it's ready to be crafted.

Sometimes a way of translating what is startling or painful is to make a metaphor. T. S. Eliot calls this the objective correlative, where an image from the outside world carries the meaning of the world inside. Let your mind rest on something that's difficult for you; see what images come to mind that might be connected. Write them down quickly, put them in a drawer, and make a date with yourself to look at them again in one month or two or three.

Fall in Love at Least Three Times a Day

I LEAVE the apartment at eight in the morning to buy groceries. I'm still a little sleepy—the rushing traffic, pounding jackhammers, and grinding garbage trucks assault me. I'm irritated by the ceaseless noise but glad today is a day to write. The sun, which before was hidden behind apartment buildings, suddenly blazes down Columbus Avenue. Blinding light shines on stacked apples, kiwis, and oranges at the corner market. The light makes the green fire hydrant look iridescent, people have haloes. I remember one of Matthew Fox's new commandments: "Thou shalt fall in love at least three times a day."

I'm in love with this light and everything the sun brushes. I look around for what else I can fall in love with. The tulips, orchids, and roses in water buckets, and the man who tends them—changing water and snipping buds. Inside, the market walls are stacked high with vegetables—unhusked corn, ripe tomatoes, the green and red next to each other make my eyes dance. I find myself whistling above the noise as I walk home carrying two heavy bags.

Matthew Fox writes:

We could fall in love with a star, of which there are 200 billion in our galaxy alone. Or a species of wildflower, of which there are at least 10,000 on this planet. Or a species of bird, of tree, of plant. Or with another human being—preferably one different from ourselves or suffering differently, such as a Salvadoran, if one is North American and prone to make war on El Salvador. Or a homosexual, if one is proud of being heterosexual. Or black, if one is white, and vice versa. We could fall in love with music, poetry, painting, dance. If we fell in love with one of Mozart's works each week, we would have seven years of joy. How could we ever be bored?

Falling in love each day expands the boundaries of love beyond my immediate family and close friends to strangers, trees, light, everything in the world, so that I can come to writing with more openness.

Each day for one week fall in love at least three times. Write it down—describe in detail what you fall in love with. What is the feeling that comes over you when you experience this falling in love? Each time we fall in love something that before was closed inside us opens and creativity begins to flow.

From an Onion to My Grandmother

A YEAR after my ninety-nine-year-old grandmother died I was sitting in the kitchen, drinking tea and staring fixedly at the table, on which were a few onions. I began to write in my journal about the onion in front of me: skin like paper, like the layers of rock in the Grand Canyon, layers of skin, my grandmother's soft papery hands, my grandmother buried in the layers of earth and bone and other lives, my grandmother's face looking up out of the earth, her skin frozen. . . .

When I finished I sat back a little startled. How had this journey happened—from an onion to my grandmother? I hadn't known I was still mourning my grandmother's death—but as I began to write about the onion I uncovered my grief. That morning I hadn't planned to write about my grandmother, let alone imagine her in a grave—but writing forged its own way through my psyche.

For many writers, freewriting or stream-of-consciousness writing is the way to find the trail. This is especially true if we have negative memories of someone's harsh criticism, if we have writer's block, if we're afraid to write what we really feel, if we've lived the life of daily chores too intensely, or if we have lots of ideas but don't know how to begin.

Pick a word—a noun, something concrete—and put it at the top of the page. It could be an arbitrary word: Onion. Feather. River. Sponge. *Or it could be something you need to think more deeply about:* Father. Time. Love. *Now begin to write everything that comes into your mind. Keep at it for at least two pages. Let yourself wander; anything—especially if it's bizarre and crazy—goes. Follow the path, and don't be afraid if it veers off somewhere else. Afterward, go back and jot down next to your freewriting the links, the journey from one thought to another. Uncover the connections that you made. After all, writing is meandering—sometimes a stroll, sometimes a fast walk—to a place of dreams, memories, and thoughts you didn't know existed.*

The Fire Within:
Writing from Anger

ON THE Big Island of Hawai'i the goddess Pele had been angered once again and was throwing her fiery lava over the earth from Mount Kilauea. We drove one evening, following the scorched earth of Pele's anger along the blue shoreline. The land smoky and burnt as after a great fire, trees charred, liquid black rock beginning to harden. We drove until we reached a barricade, got out of the car, and walked half a mile farther to get a closer view of the lava river flowing across the road and into the sea. We could see steam rising where the sea and the lava met. Everything along the lava's path— houses, trees, animals—had been turned to stone and ashes.

Fifty people sat quietly on rocks, witnessing the creation of new earth. We joined them, mesmerized by the thick fire stream flowing slowly but steadily toward the Pacific, flaring as the ocean leapt up and swept pieces of lava into the sea where they became floating torches. Night descended, the only sounds the breaking waves, the hissing lava, and a few whispers.

That night I thought about Pele's anger. For thousands of years Pele has periodically gotten angry enough to open Mount Kilauea and hurl molten rock. For thousands of years the Hawai'ian people have tried to appease her with offerings. Pele is a powerful metaphor for anger—as both destroyer and creator: everything that lies in her path is devastated at the same time she creates a new shoreline for the southern coast of Hawai'i.

Anger is a tremendous source of creativity. I often overlook anger as a source for writing because I'm afraid of that power locked inside me. Emily Dickinson uses the volcano/anger metaphor in this poem:

> On my volcano grows the Grass
> A meditative spot—
> An acre for a Bird to choose
> Would be the General thought—
>
> How red the Fire rocks below—
> How insecure the sod
> Did I disclose
> Would populate with awe my solitude.

Much powerful writing comes from anger. In this fine poem by Abelardo Delgado, we feel the "Fire rocks below" the words:

Stupid America

> stupid america, see that chicano
> with a big knife
> in his steady hand
> he doesn't want to knife you
> he wants to sit on a bench
> and carve christ figures

but you won't let him.
stupid america, hear that chicano
shouting curses on the street
he is a poet
without paper and pencil
and since he cannot write
he will explode.
stupid america, remember that chicanito
flunking math and english
he is the picasso
of your western states
but he will die
with one thousand masterpieces
hanging only from his mind.

Release the anger inside you by writing about it. You can address it to whomever or whatever angers you. Be truthful . . . let all the words that come from anger emerge—don't hold back. You can curse, call names, threaten, whatever you need to do to release this anger. Anger is a source of creativity. In this exercise, you and Pele are working together.

Ten Observations a Day

MARIE AND I were talking about writing. She said, "According to Keats, 'a poet is the most unpoetical of any thing in existence; because he has no identity.' The other day I was looking out the window of my apartment toward the roof of that billion-dollar townhouse and I saw three pigeons fighting; two were pecking a third. They pecked and pecked and pecked until finally the pigeon being pecked flapped its wings and the other two flew off, and it stood there proud and dark by itself. Those people in the house had no idea what was going on on their roof. I bet I was the only one who saw it. Then all the pigeons flew down and landed on the top of a lamppost. I hadn't realized before that the top of a lamp was a place for pigeons. You know, we have places where we go, but this was a place for them."

We talked about how, to be writers, we have to be able to sit at the window and unbecome ourselves. As we're staring out the window at the pigeons we must become them, we must leave our world and enter theirs. We must lose our personalities and become receptors for the world. We must become what we see. That's why our unmediated observations of the world become the foundation for writing. In Marie's writing workshop she has her students write ten observations a day. Without commentary. These observations become touchstones for much of their writing later on. Marie is teaching her students how to live like writers.

Every day for a week write ten observational sketches in your notebook. Take a walk and write what you notice; describe the sounds you hear in or outside your house or apartment. Write these sketches quickly and with no judgment, no editorializing. The more accurately you can observe your world and capture it in words, the more concrete your writing will become.

Layers

AT DINNER one night last week Suzanne asked me, "What is the one image that you think represents your life?" I immediately said, "Layers." "As in phyllo dough?" (There is a baker lurking in Suzanne.) "No. As in the Grand Canyon."

Layers: of rocks; of a Native American burial ground in the Northeast; of the excavated ancient Roman city of Gallop in Saint Rémy, a few hundred feet from where Van Gogh stood painting, unaware of the wonders beneath him; of the ancient city of Pompeii. When I visit these places I am haunted by, obsessed with, the idea of layers. But it's not just the layers of rock or earth that I'm fascinated by; it's the search through the layers, which will lead me to important truths about my life.

Rilke writes: "Work of the eyes is done, now / go and do heartwork / on all the images imprisoned within you; / for you overpowered them: / but even now you don't know them." What recurring images do I notice in my writing, in my memories? Finding these key images is crucial and important work for me as a writer.

The seemingly random observations I make or the subjects I choose to write about are like the branches of a tree whose roots reach down to the depths of myself and reveal my obsessions.

These images also serve another function. As Robert Bly writes, "The image always holds to one of the senses at least, to smell or taste or touch or hearing, the seeing of color or motion. If one says, 'The good of one is the good of all,' one abandons the senses almost successfully. . . . The image moistens the poem . . . with certain energies that do not flow from a source in our personal life. Without that moistness the poem becomes dry or stuck in one world."

The task of finding your key images is lifework. But you can begin with a few questions: Are there any images that keep coming back to you in your writing or in your memories? Do you see any patterns in what you choose to write about? Have you noticed any themes that keep recurring in your journal? As you're writing try to remain aware of the images that are significant for you.

First Memory

My sister and I are swinging on the swing sets in Texas. The sky is darkening; in the west it scowls a greenish black. The winds have started. My mother stands next to our small brick house on the base, her hair and skirt blowing, calling our names to come in. I hop off my swing and turn around to wait for my sister. She swings higher and higher, her legs sticking out straight in front of her. A tornado is coming. My mother can hardly walk now because the wind is so strong. She walks toward my sister, who jumps off the swing, spraining her ankle. My mother carries her in her arms, and I follow behind.

This is the first conscious imprint on my mind. I was five and my father was in the army and stationed in Texas. A tornado was approaching and my sister wouldn't come inside. From the time I was born until that afternoon I had lived five years but I can't remember anything. What happened to these memories? This first memory is significant to me, the fact that I remember it at all. A storm coming. Perhaps I felt something in the air—my parents' eventual divorce, my tumultuous relationship with my sister when we were children.

I wonder if a first remembered image is like the language of a dream—a blueprint of deeper feelings and intuitions. Our first images seem like myths, stories we tell ourselves for years, the details polished over time. Stanley Kunitz writes: "We have to go back and reconstruct the foundation myths, so they will live again for us. Poetry is tied to memory. . . . Poetry is ultimately mythology, the telling of the stories of the soul." A first memory is the first story embedded on the soul.

Write down your first memory. Let the story gestate, then ask your-self what's underneath it—is there any significance to this image in your current life? If so, write about this connection and see where it leads you.

Rivers of Memory

WHEN I was a girl, our house in Virginia was built on a creek's flood plain. That first summer after we moved in, the August rains came—days of thunderstorms and sheeted rain—and the creek remembered, rose over its banks, into our yard, down into the stairwell, knocked the back door in, and settled in our house. The creek's memory returned two summers in a row, until the town decided they had better build a dam to try to hold it. The developers had no business building in the creek's way, where it had flooded for hundreds of years.

Toni Morrison writes:

> The act of imagination is bound up with memory. You know, they straightened out the Mississippi River in places, to make room for houses and livable acreage. Occasionally, the river floods these places. "Floods" is the word they use, but in fact it is not flooding; it is remembering . . . what valley we ran through, what the banks were like, the light that was there and the route back to our original place. It is emotional memory—what the nerves and the skin remember as well as how it appeared. And a rush of imagination is our "flooding."

Sometimes a memory will come surging back from child-hood at some unexpected moment, as I'm climbing the flight of stairs up to the apartment or chopping vegetables or driving along a highway. Memory's cloak is usually an image, something I can see or taste or hear or feel. Whenever I smell molasses, I remember my grandmother baking molasses cookies in her kitchen in New Hampshire, the click of her high heels on the linoleum floor, my grandfather's clocks ticking and chiming on the hour, a whippoorwill calling at dusk from the deep woods, as if it were happening right now.

One of the best ways to write about memories is by speaking them aloud. For this exercise, you'll need a partner or, if that's impossible, you can use a tape recorder. First, think of a memory from childhood: it can be a significant life-changing memory or an ordinary one. Now speak this memory as you see it (or taste, smell, hear, or touch it) to your partner or into the tape recorder. Don't explain, just trust the memory. Your partner will write down what you're saying exactly as you say it, including any words you repeat for emphasis. Stop when you think you've spoken your memory completely. Have your partner read what you said back to you. (If you're speaking into a tape recorder, transcribe exactly what you've said.) Is there anything you left out? Tell this to your partner or add it to the tape.

Now, ask yourself these questions: What's significant to me about this memory? What made me think of this particular memory today? Sometimes analyzing the image adds another layer to it. Soaked with memory's image, the writing from this exercise can't help but be vivid and concrete.

The Full Picture

ON A summer day in my memory I am a girl playing horses with Mary near the creek and the honeysuckle smells sweet and the creek sings and I am very happy.

This is the way I'd like to remember my childhood. But this is only part of the story. I also remember that both my father and Mary's father were in Vietnam during the most dangerous time of the war, my father a helicopter pilot, and how we couldn't speak about it because we had no language for it. Our mothers didn't talk about it to themselves or to their daughters; so we whinnied and pawed the ground with our hooves and named our horses after the helicopters my father flew and used a kind of animal sign language to communicate with each other.

Judith Ortiz-Cofer:

> As one gets older, childhood years are often conveniently consolidated into one perfect summer's afternoon. The events can be projected on a light blue screen; the hurtful parts can be edited out, and the moments of joy brought in sharp focus to the foreground. It is our show. But with all that on the cutting room floor, what remains to tell?

Even an idyllic childhood, which seems to be unusual, has within it losses and fears, the small and sometimes profound tragedies of children, who have so little control over their lives.

When we write about our childhood—about anything, for that matter—we need to make sure that we write the full picture, include the storm clouds as well as the blue sky, the trees' shadow silhouetted on the ground as well as the tree. Sometimes when we read writing that has edited out the full range of emotions present in everyday life, including the life of a child, we can smell the perfume trying to cover something up. It's too strong, too sweet, and we don't believe it.

Return to a moment, a memory, a day in your childhood. Picture it so clearly you can almost touch it. Divide your page in half. In the first column, write about this day, this image, in the dewy light of nostalgia—make the sun shine, pretend everything is pleasant. In other words, play it in C major, no flats or sharps. In the second column expand your range. Include any foreboding, fears, shadows, doubts, thoughts that make this image, this scene, more complex and nuanced than the first version. Read them both. Look at them side by side and compare the two worlds. Which feels more true? Would blending the two describe the truth more accurately?

Visual Archaeology

My mother holds me upright in her arms, there is a distance between our bodies. Her hair is black except for the ribbon of grey. She's smiling and holding a cigarette. I'm two, and stare worriedly at the camera—my father—holding a shell in my clutched fingers, which are silhouetted on my mother's chest like a shadow game. Behind us, the sea unfolds, steel grey. An unknown woman sits in a chair near the waves looking out. The dark army blanket is spread out on the sand . . .

Each day I walk by this black-and-white photograph of an ordinary day at the beach with my parents. It is a window into my childhood. Yet this photograph—this pose, me in my mother's arms—will exist longer than either of us. In the photo, my mother is younger than I am now, and I'm beginning to resemble her more and more.

When I look at photographs of my childhood, I am gathering shards of the past, trying to make meaning out of its fragments. Sometimes they bring back a forgotten moment: the time at the Sandwich Fair when I ate caramel apples; me in my new strawberry dress and hat; my best friend's dog, Laddie. Photographs make me laugh or remember with a stab of regret. Photographs demand that stories be told around them.

Sebastião Salgado, one of the greatest photographers of our time, calls his photographs visual archaeology. For his book *Workers* he photographed men and women using their hands. There are photographs of cocoa workers, miners, and men and women who pick tobacco and roll cigars. His preface is like the accompaniment to a song:

> Working with tobacco is sweet and gentle. It can be compared to making bread: it is ancient, meticulous, exact, unique work. . . . The leaves are collected almost ceremoniously. The baskets are lined with cloth like warm cradles, and the leaves are placed inside them like sleeping babies. And while the hands work, the cigars grow to the sound of poems, words, and songs. The room is large and airy and, in front of the cigar makers, a person sits whose job it is to read aloud. He gently scatters words that help the mind travel while fingers and palms gently roll the cigars, the leaves capturing the dreams that will rise in clouds of smoke.

Salgado reminds me that it's the viewer who brings photographs to life. My insistence on making meaning, telling stories, remembering and piecing together the past, can inspire writing. Writing about photographs is a way to take the pieces of the past and reconstruct a face, a family, a town, a life.

Find a photograph of yourself as a child—it can be of you alone or it can include other people. Run your eyes over it. Write down quickly

everything you think and feel. Sometimes description only lets you wander around outside the window looking in. One way to become part of the photograph's world, to go more deeply into it, is to imagine yourself speaking as the child you were. What would you say? What would you hear or smell?

You can also find a photograph of something in the world—from the newspaper, old magazines, photographs you've seen repeatedly that have become icons of a certain time or situation. Find a photograph that resonates emotionally for you. Remember, the point is not just to write a description but to drift, dream, let poetry happen, let images connect you deeply to what you see.

Layers of History

I ARRIVED in Manassas in the late afternoon the day before I was to give a workshop at a local high school. I grew up in Virginia, not too far from there, and knew this was Civil War battlefield country. Next to the Battlefield Courtyard Marriott, where I was staying, was the Battleview Business Park: neatly mown lawns, perfectly trimmed hedges, newly pruned trees surrounded by wood chips, and a building made of tinted glass. No sign of any battle here, nor any sign of people, since it was after five and everyone had gone for the day. I inquired at the hotel's front desk, and the woman there directed me along the main road for about a mile—to the site of the Battle of Henry Hill at Bull Run.

The sky's blue was deepening, a storm approached; I heard thunder in the distance as I walked along the shoulder of the highway, cars rushing past. When I arrived at the battle site, the parking lot was empty; it was dusk and any minute ready to pour. I stood on the hill overlooking the battlefield. A map outlined where the fighting took place, where each side was positioned: some soldiers hid behind that clump of trees to the right, some lay in the hollow to the left, and the small stone house directly in front in the valley, that's where they took the wounded. The thunder rumbled and lightning flashed, and suddenly I was there among smoking cannons, the moans and cries of wounded boys, bloody bodies strewn on the grass. And I was terrified. The dead had come to life. The contrast of the imagined battle with the peaceful green hills and the rushing commuters driving home from work became startling clear.

I ran back to the hotel in the rain. While I paused in the lobby to catch my breath, the woman at the front desk told me that recently some businesspeople had wanted to build a mall on the battlefield, but the local residents raised a ruckus and won. I went back to my room and, still drenched, got out some paper:

Battleview

On the site of the Battle of Henry Hill where mounds
    of earth rise and fall,
the grass is stained with the blood of soldiers—
not twenty yards from here, the sign says.

Crickets scratch back and forth as if answering questions
the dead have: why were they cut down early
and like this on this hill?

The sign says: Here in July 1861, in the place where
    we stand,
you could hear the deafening sounds of artillery—as
    thunder marbles
the sky, and mist rolls across the trees like the smoke
    of cannons.

What happened over a hundred years ago still bleeds
    through—

don't pretend that it doesn't. Your Battleview Business
    Park:
paved roads, planted trees, and wood chip paths don't
    mask the ghosts.

The Courtyard Marriott, on the edge of the battlefield,
    is lit orange,
against the blueing sky. As I walk along the road, men
    in trucks yell
Hey Baby as crickets hop frantically out of the way.

Stiff grass scratches my ankles; with each step, I hear
    the battle
fade. What would have become of those young men,
who would be dead anyway, if they hadn't died here
    so young:

perhaps they would have spent the rest of their lives
    as farmers,
or fathers of children, or walking down a dusty road
    beside a wagon
carrying goods to a town, or crossing the
    Rappahannock on a ferry?

Let's build a mall here. It's all sewn up. That was then—
there is no more battle. Let's build on top.
But the living cried out:

the dead are our cherished selves, our children.
And the rattling skies whitened the land with even
    more heat.

The land has layers of history beneath it; part of our
job as writers is to become sensitive to the ghosts, the past,

the history underneath the lives we lead and the land we lead them on. Jimmy Santiago Baca says, "[The writing] journey begins in the landscape we were given; the place where we were born is our point of departure. New Mexico's mountains, deserts, plains, and barrios, rivers and ditches, fields and yards, initiated me in my craft." The rolling hills of Virginia and the ghosts of Civil War battles were all part of my childhood. My friends and I roamed the then-undeveloped ninety acres of woods behind our houses and found old bullets and nails from houses now gone; our childhood play was infused with the history of the land we grew up on.

Write in the voice of the land you currently live on or were born on. What happened there? What was happening five hundred years ago? Describe what the land has seen. You might need to do a little research about the land that grew you and the people who lived there before you.

Gannon Hill

AFTER FIVE hours of driving, our family station wagon climbed the dirt road up toward Gannon Hill—my godparents' house in upstate New York. This was our annual summer stopover on our trip to my grandparents' house in New Hampshire. Gannon Hill was what my godparents called their white clapboard house with evergreen shutters. The house faced what were to me the mysterious Catskill Mountains, where Rip Van Winkle slept for a hundred years. I remember standing on that hill searching for him in the distant blue, certain that one of these years I would spot him.

Gannon Hill was a place where I felt truly loved. Maybe it was this love that made the house seem magical. The bedroom where my sisters and I slept was decorated with floral wallpaper, there were lace doilies on the dresser with crystal perfume bottles on them. But the doll room was my dream come true. When Aunt Marjorie was a girl she began to collect dolls, and she continued throughout her life. There were china-faced dolls, dolls almost as tall as a seven-year-old, dolls dressed in velvet coats and white gloves, baby dolls in carriages, dolls confined to the "doll hospital" (one had belonged to my aunt when she was a girl and had a face worn thin and split down the middle). In the center of the room was Aunt Marjorie's dollhouse: when she took the front off I sat mesmerized before it, my eyes walking from room to room. The table was set for Thanksgiving, complete with miniature candelabra (with candles), knives, forks, and napkins. One bedroom had a canopied bed and a Persian rug; the kitchen pantry was filled with small cans of food. I wanted to live in that dollhouse, and on one night each summer, I did.

I felt cherished at Gannon Hill; everything was all right with the world there, and with me. It was a fantasy world, filled with endlessly fascinating treasures, where I was welcomed.

There were other times as a child when I felt this way. Each Sunday afternoon my mother made the big meal of the day. Sometimes we'd have a traditional southern meal of ham, grits, and red-eyed gravy with biscuits, other times a turkey, or roast beef and Yorkshire pudding. I'd be up in my room reading *The Secret Garden* and the house smelled safe and good and delicious.

These happy memories have been important for me to remember as I also do the work that so many writers do of excavating the times that didn't feel like this.

Do you have a memory of one place in childhood where you felt completely welcomed and loved? It doesn't have to be your own home; perhaps it was the home of a neighbor, a grandmother or grandfather, an aunt or an uncle, or maybe it was in a library, under a favorite tree, or at school—a place where the world seemed cheerful and safe. Describe this place in abundant detail.

Stones and Sorrow

WHEN YOU hold a stone in your hand you are holding the history of the earth: wind blasting on a fall night, sun, cold winters, rainstorms, the sound of river water flowing over rocks—the story of the natural world made manifest. All of us hold the history of our lives, as well as our ancestors' and the world's history, inside us. Memories darkened by ages of forgetting are still inside somewhere hiding, waiting for the right smell or touch to unlock them. Susan Griffin says, "For perhaps we are like stones; our own history and the history of the world embedded in us, we hold a sorrow deep within and cannot weep until that history is sung."

All of our lives know deep sorrows and ecstatic joys and a hundred nuanced emotions in between. But sometimes this United States culture wants to drown sorrow in Smiley Faces and "Don't Worry Be Happy" songs; we don't allow ourselves to feel sorrow without feeling ashamed that there's something wrong with us. Millions of people drink or spend their lives in front of televisions to avoid feeling pain.

I hold a great sorrow in me now about the growing number of people living on the streets. I see the disparity between rich and poor widening. In my fifteen-year relationship with New York City, the homeless have multiplied, and the 1990s are a time of retribution and hardened hearts.

If we could see the history of our ancestors' emotional lives, the world's lives, in gradations of colors like the layers of the Grand Canyon, we would see many shades of sorrow. But we try to hide our grief. We are like the stone we hold in our hand, full of stories and voiceless, waiting for our history to be sung.

Trace the layers of your life; is there any unresolved sorrow or grief still lingering somewhere inside you, closed like a winter bud? Hidden sorrows turn into secrets, which, like tumors, grow bigger and can drain your joy, your creativity. Write about a sorrow you feel. Once you've allowed it to breathe, it will begin to lose its secret power, stop tugging at your psyche to pay attention.

Listening to the Corn

I SAT in the sand by a cornfield near Peter's Pond and closed my eyes. Late summer, and the crickets orchestrated their rusty raspings in the grass. A strong wind from the ocean pushed against the green corn stalks, and the corn whispered back. It wasn't a language I was familiar with, so it took me a while to figure out how to listen. It wasn't speaking words exactly, but its own language. The day was warm, the sky blue, but the slight chill of fall was in the air. The corn was becoming drier, the crickets louder, as if like the leaves in fall they needed to blast their sounds before dying. I sat by the cornfield for a long time listening to the corn murmur that summer was over.

The corn that day reminded me of the mescal agave plant and the words of a Yaqui song performed by Don Jesus Yoilo'i, a distinguished Yaqui deer singer: "Still I am beautiful / with green leaves / sitting / toward the top / I have black fruit / standing." Don Jesus says, "The mescal agave talks like that when it's almost dying." The Yaqui song honors the life and sacrifice of the mescal agave; the survival of the people of the Sonoran desert depended on it.

That September day out in the cornfield I slowed down

enough to listen to what the corn was saying. The earth has its own language. Driving to the grocery store, hopping off buses and onto planes, I can't hear much of anything except the noise of engines.

Go for a walk. Listen to the streets, fields, or trees, whatever is around you. Try to hear what the world is telling you. Now try writing in the voice of what you are listening to or seeing: the street, shadows, birds, footsteps, trees.

In That Time

I ALWAYS wonder what people hundreds of years from now will think about the lives we're leading now; as our planet is dying and inhumanity is becoming the political wave of the future, I still get in my car and drive where I need to go or walk past a homeless man huddled under blankets on a Central Park bench or watch from my window as a boy of ten searches with his father through garbage cans at night, the windchill outside nine degrees, as I sit in my warm apartment reading a book. I wonder at my capacity to witness all this suffering without going crazy and without taking action.

Jimmy Santiago Baca writes:

> The writer must be free to go crazy, whether with ecstasy or pain, to explode the indifference of a world that accepts that "home" for some families is a nest of cardboard boxes, that accepts such abominations. The writer must be free to delve into the offensive and the vile, to rut in the mud as in the flowers, and to challenge with the truth of his vision and experience the keepers of the lie and the wielders of oppression, no matter where they are found.

We live every day witnessing the injustices and tragedies of our world: oil spills ravaging lands and waters, soaking birds and other animals with poison; toxins knowingly dumped near neighborhoods where, afterward, the rate of child leukemia skyrockets; shootings that have become an ordinary occurrence with too easily accessible guns. Any one of us could go on and on about stories she's heard, he's heard, and all of us, even if we try to block it out, feel the pain.

Bertolt Brecht once said that people would ask about Germans during World War II, "Why were their poets silent?" It is a writer's job to act as a witness to the world, to remind us all to stay awake.

Suzanne has written a series of poems called "In That Time," from the perspective of a years-into-the-future history books. Here's one of them:

In That Time

In that time the people presided over
what came to be known as The Great Dying
Osprey and herons and hawks were exchanged
for speedboats and paved wooden neighborhoods
Bear and beaver and moose disappeared
for top hats and gas pumps to take their places
The gifts to the seventh generation
included dead fish piled in simmering creeks
tides that bore surgical sutures and needles
horizons heavy with smokestacks and tailpipes
falling on trees as searing rain
The earth was opened for interment of poisons
The sky was divided by lots and sold
The sounds that the wind and rain made together
became audible only in fenced preserves
Unprecedented prosperity

sustained the industries of destruction
the makers of stacks of prison cages
of chairs designed for electrocution
of weapons to suppurate the deserts
and erase waterlines and warehouses of seeds
A banner of that time depicts many children
standing on top of a map of the world
Some smile Some stare without expression
at the thicket of swords hanging over their heads

Begin writing with the phrase "In that time . . ." and write in the voice of the future, as if it were two hundred years from now and you're looking back to these difficult days. Be specific—describe what you witness every day that is painful and unjust.

The Family in the Next Booth

NEXT TO me at the Omega Diner, I noticed four people scrunched into a booth made for two, all of them wearing dark colors: a small girl named Alexandra wearing a purple dress, lying down; her father, balding and harried, with a Brooklyn accent; a woman with white hair and a face filled with grief; and a woman with auburn hair, who was not Alexandra's mother, whose lap Alexandra stretched out in. Eavesdropping, I deduced that they were waiting to attend a funeral at the mortuary across the street. Alexandra's grandmother had died. The elderly woman said to Alexandra, "Why don't you sit up?" Alexandra replied, "I don't want to sit up. I'm tired." They ordered one cheese Danish among them, three plates, and a hot chocolate for Alexandra.

I continued eating my breakfast, listening with one ear. Alexandra said, "How am I going to say good-bye to Grandma when she's in a box?" There was a long silence. The auburn-haired woman said gently, "Well, you can try and remember what she looked like, and when you touch the box that's when you can say good-bye to her." Alexandra lay down again and was silent.

My heart couldn't help but open to these four strangers,

who didn't seem like strangers at all by the time I left the diner but kin in some larger, more universal way. I cared deeply about how Alexandra was going to have to face death that day and understood the tired, gentle silence of the adults at the table. My glimpses into strangers' lives expand my compassion for other people and deepen my understanding of the larger world.

Wherever you go, let yourself get caught up in other people's stories. Become aware of how your mind begins to create stories around them, filling in the gaps you don't know. Write down conversations you overhear, fragments of people's dialogue that you catch as you stroll down the street. You never know when these conversations will want to appear in your writing.

Back from the Mountains,
a Yellow Handrail

I WALKED briskly along Forty-second Street, on the way to a friend's play, past the blinking neon signs: Live, Live Girls, Private Viewing Booths, The Nugget, Flame Steaks, Amigo Cameras & Electronics. Outside, men stood on the sidewalk, hands in pockets, gazing at passersby. Muslim men in front of white-clothed tables sold incense, books, and oils, the air perfumed for a moment. I glanced quickly at the marquee for the Empire Theater. I expected to see more advertising, but did a double take: black letters spelled these words, all in capital letters: SUNLIGHT SHINES RED / THROUGH MY FATHER'S THUMB / ON THE STEERING WHEEL.

I stopped. Had I read it right? I backed up, read it again, and then glanced at another marquee further down the street: BACK FROM THE MOUNTAINS / A YELLOW HANDRAIL GUIDES ME / DOWN THE SUBWAY STAIRS.

Haiku on Forty-second Street? What was going on? Every marquee on this stretch of street offered a different poem: ALMOST FULL MOON / A LUXURIOUS VOICE / ON THE ANSWERING MACHINE and FIRST SNOW / BROUGHT IN FROM THE SUBURBS / ON THE NEIGHBORS' CAR.

Later I discovered that this was the work of Creative

Time, Inc., and the 42nd Street Development Project, organizations committed to displaying art in public spaces and to "encourag[ing] audiences to OPEN THEIR IMAGINATIONS and discover the buried treasure that lies beneath the glitter . . . of this celebrated streetscape." All of the haiku on the marquees were chosen and the display installed by Dee Evetts, a haiku poet in New York. Most of the poets were members of the Haiku Society of America, Inc. The haiku added a layer of beauty to the abandoned theatres and to the many sad and desperate faces I walked by that night— the urban landscape transformed.

On the next block the marquees switched back to Adult Video, Girls Girls Girls, Live Sex, Models. I missed the poems that had kept me company as I walked, so I began to write my own: WHAT DOES IT MEAN / TO SELL / A KISS?

In no time I arrived at my friend's play.

Write a series of haiku in one sitting. Don't belabor them—and don't worry about the form—spin these observations and moments off your pen in three short lines as quickly and accurately as possible. The beauty of a haiku is its brevity; it teaches you to use words more clearly and truthfully.

Whispering into the Air

IN 1968 my father left for three months at a time to fly helicopters in Vietnam. Each week my mother, sisters, and I sat down on the floor in my parents' bedroom and spoke into a tape recorder, and my mother would send the tape to my father in Saigon. We each had only a few minutes to speak. I told him about ice skating on the C & O canal, about my passing report card, about my birthday slumber party. I asked him about the monkey he had adopted and named after my sister, how he was doing, and when he was coming back. These tapes were like letters, but more immediate, because we knew he'd be hearing our real voices. I didn't realize it then, but we were using an ancient figure of speech called an apostrophe.

Apostrophe comes literally from the Greek, 'to turn away.' An actor in ancient Greece might turn away from the audience and address someone who was not on stage, someone absent or dead. It's not just a whispering into the air; although the person might not be there, what you say is meant for him or her to hear. As a figure of speech, it sweetens writing with an intimacy it might not otherwise have and enables us to speak the truth to a person we might not be able to address if he were really there in front of us. I often tell my students to pretend they're speaking to a good friend; it grounds the writing and makes it more direct and intimate.

One of the first poems I wrote was about my father's time in Vietnam. I began it in the third person: "He was standing in the dusk . . ." but it wasn't working. When I began to speak directly to my father, as I did through the tape recorder years ago, the poem finally came together.

To the Memory Of

You were standing in the dusk
as evening was painting night on the
    trees.
The pine needles were open:
    sea-coral, spiked anemones,
gold, lucky like a clatter of coins,
before midnight loomed over you.
You were like a soldier waiting,
    expecting to die.

The water was peacock blue.
The white porcelain rattle
that rose and fell in the loon's voice
was solitary and loose on the water,
revealing the invisible
like white feathers in the white air.

I fear the pulse of water at dusk,
lashing the stones
like a bird struggling nervous, helpless.

You turning away,
pulling me under without will.
The impulse broken by the wilderness
collapsing in you.

Write an apostrophe. Address it to someone with whom you would like to speak and to whom you have something important to say. The person can be alive or dead. Speak honestly. Tell that person what's important. What's on your mind and heart. How you feel. Maybe there's something unresolved between you. Maybe you want an intimacy with the person that you don't have and here's your chance to tell this person how you feel. Perhaps you're angry or hurt and you haven't been able to express that.

Another version of this is to write to something inanimate: a tree, a river, the stars, a city. Speak to the things of this world as if they could hear you.

Ancestors

BOTH MY maternal and paternal grandfathers were generals in the army; before that my great-grandfather was a general as well. One grandfather wrote his memoirs, *The Pictorial Military History of Jack Whitehead Heard:* years after he died I read it, trying to piece together his life, and the lives of his father and mother before him. Through my grandfather's words, as well as through photographs and remembered stories, my ancestors began to speak.

What was it like for my paternal grandfather to fly an early plane with linen wings and to be one of the first to discover how to loop in the air after his friends had tried the loop and crashed and died? For my grandmother to grow up in Eagle Pass, Texas, and to have her father die when she was twelve? For my maternal grandmother to have married four times, the first time at sixteen? For my paternal grandfather to grow up on a tobacco farm in North Carolina and, as a boy, to have his father shoot himself?

Malidoma Patrice Somé believes that much of the sickness of modern society is the result of our disowning or being ignorant of our ancestors and their lives. He writes: "The Dagara believe that it is the duty of the living to heal their ancestors. If these ancestors are not healed, their sick energy will haunt the souls and psyches of those who are responsible for helping them." Most of us have some idea who our grandparents and even our great-grandparents were, but beyond that many of us have lost contact. The voices of our ancestors are within us; we may share the same language, hair, facial expressions, body gestures, propensity for alcohol, or dreams.

Walt Whitman writes in his preface to *Leaves of Grass*:

> Past and present and future are not disjointed but joined. The greatest poet forms the consistence of what is to be from what has been and is. He drags the dead out of their coffins and stands them again on their feet. . . . He says to the past, Rise and walk before me that I may realize you.

Choose one of your ancestors to whom you feel close. Write and speak to this person. What would you say? What questions would they ask you? What would they see? What would they say to you?

Synchronicity:
Connecting the World

I WAS drinking coffee in the Broadway Diner and writing about my father's time in Vietnam. After I finished I was exhausted, so I stared out the window, watching the rain stream down, thinking about how much I love snow and how it never snows in New York anymore. When I left, I jumped in a cab, and the driver and I complained about the weather. I said, "I love snow. Ever since I was a girl and we had a blizzard and everything was shut down for weeks I've loved snow." The cab driver said, "Well, I was just telling my wife this morning how special snow is to me because of the blizzard of 1966." I remembered the big snowstorm that year. "That's the year I was supposed to go to Vietnam," he said, "and because all the airports were closed here my unit left without nine of us. We were sent to Korea instead. Out of the 179 men who went to Vietnam, 160 died." As he wove through the Manhattan streets we talked more about Vietnam. When I arrived at my destination I stepped out of the cab, never to see this man again, but I knew we were meant to connect that afternoon.

Jung researched and then wrote an essay about synchronicity: how seemingly unconnected events become con-

nected by a kind of "meaningful cross-connection." Our lives
are connected to one another's and to the larger world and
universe. Sometimes I have doubts or questions about my
life, and the world seems to answer back with connection:
migrating starlings flock in the trees after my grandfather
dies, or I'm wondering how a friend is and the phone rings
and there she is.

I wrote a poem about a true synchronistic event in my life:

The Visit

The week my grandfather died,
the shadow of a strange bird,
wings wide as an eagle's,
swept across the grass.
Starlings came to light in the trees,
hundreds of them blackened the branches
outside the window, squawking their metallic
    chants for hours.
A hawk sitting on the highway sign
turned its head as I drove by.
The birds were a sign from my grandfather,
come to tell me that the dead don't stay scattered
and meaningless, but change
and give signs to the living,
like when I was a girl
surprised to find the random numbered dots
connected by a line
change into a tree or a house.
This morning, raking leaves from the crocuses,
I uncovered the perfect white skeleton of a
    grackle,
bones almost translucent, thin legs folded beneath,
skull and beak pressed in the dirt.

Synchronicity draws recognizable patterns on a some-times chaotic universe. Writers need to pay attention to these synchronistic moments and events.

On my first night in the house where I live in Sag Harbor there was a huge thunderstorm; a tree in the back-yard, one of the oldest trees in town, was struck by lightning and part of it fell on the power lines to the roof, waking us. A good omen? A welcome or a warning from the household gods? A sign from the spirits? Now I look out the window at that same silver maple and remember that first night here when it was felled by lightning. New shoots and branches are growing up from its rotting trunk, and I feel inspired at the strength of the will to live and grow.

Be on the lookout for moments that connect. Write them down when they happen. Once you begin to look for them, you'll find more and more of these connections, until you'll count on them as part of your life. Sometimes writing becomes too predictable—the reader knows what you'll say before you even say it. Life can seem this way too; you have a list of everything you're going to do, go to the grocery store, get a haircut. But what about what's underneath? What is the sky saying today? What does it mean that you've banged your finger three times? Write about the events of your life as signs from the universe—all connected to a larger meaning.

Metaphors emerge from this very connection. Write sentences that connect two seemingly disconnected things: a burned tree with its green shoots and your life; the overcast sky and the flu; waves and the skin on your hands. Strain a little, be a little crazy in your connections. Make a list of impossible yet interesting connections.

Dreams

SEVERAL YEARS ago, I had a dream that was so vivid I began to pay attention to all of my dreams: I wore a long, deep-burgundy velvet dress and was waiting for guests to arrive. The room was filled with roses and lilacs. My friends and family climbed the wide marble stairs to where I stood, and I announced that I was going to marry myself. People seemed pleased. The ceremony was quick. I repeated a few words to myself then hugged the guests, and we all danced. I woke up the next morning ecstatically happy.

For a long time I couldn't remember my dreams, and I felt there was something inside me that had been gagged, shut off, a window painted over. I knew that outside the window was a spectacular view of my interior life.

Dreams, as Jung knew, have their own language. It is often figurative, and similar to the figures of speech writers use. Dreams are the poet's companion. We dream in the language of poets, yet dreams are usually woven together by a narrative thread. They are mirrors we can hold up to help us sort out our feelings and wishes. Jung said, "The best way to deal with a dream is to think of yourself as a sort of ignorant child . . . and to come to a two-million-year-old man or to the old mother of days and ask, 'Now, what do you think of me?'"

When I remember my dreams I usually feel more creative and open the next day. They remind me that I have an inner life, even when I get too busy and distracted to reflect on it.

Dreams have been woven into the fabric of literature from ancient times (in epic poems like *Gilgamesh*, the *Iliad*, and the *Divine Comedy*) to today. W. H. Auden says, "Learn from your dreams what you lack."

One way to capture your dreams is in a dream journal. Keep a separate notebook and a pen by your bed, and as soon as you wake after a dream, write it down. In the afternoon, when your dreams have usually been forgotten, get out your notebook and "redream" them. Remember, dreams are windows into your inner creative life. What are they trying to tell you?

Songs to the Everyday

IMAGINE WRITING poems of praise to a tomato, a storm, clothes, a fallen chestnut, a book, a yellow bird, a wrist-watch, laziness. Pablo Neruda did just that in his odes. He exalted the everyday, the familiar things of life, and transformed this ancient form.

Ode comes from the Greek word *aeidein* meaning 'to sing' or 'to chant.' Originally, poets wrote odes to celebrate public events or to praise famous people, as Marvell did in his "Horatian Ode." The tone in an ode was serious, the diction heightened. Neruda reclaimed this form to celebrate the things we usually take for granted. Like this:

Ode to My Socks

Maru Mori brought me
a pair
of socks
knitted with her own
shepherd's hands,

two socks soft
as rabbits.
I slipped
my feet into them
as if
into
jewel cases
woven
with threads of
dusk
and sheep's wool.

Audacious socks,
my feet became
two woolen
fish,
two long sharks
of lapis blue
shot
with a golden thread,
two mammoth blackbirds,
two cannons,
thus honored
were
my
feet
by
these
celestial
socks.

My own praises to common things would include the mulberry tree outside the window that attracts birds and squirrels I can watch as I'm writing, garlic, wind, hot water, and my feet.

Write an ode (don't worry about the form), a chant, in praise of the ordinary things in your life that you feel grateful for. Choose something that's common and everyday, then exalt it.

Found Writing

HERE'S AN idea that began one cold New England August when friends came to visit in Vermont. For one week it poured and the temperature never rose above 65 degrees. We caught up on old news, made sumptuous feasts, read by the fire, and the rain continued. By the third day, we got restless. After an early supper one evening, we sat at the wooden kitchen table. Someone said, "Let's write a poem together." We all groaned. She persisted. "Let's try making found poems." We reluctantly agreed, learned the rules, and began.

We each had five minutes to gather whatever books we were able to find in the house. I ran to one bedroom and grabbed a book on the haunted houses of England, an atlas, and a bunch of old cookbooks. We piled our diverse assortments on the table and went to work: choosing sentences and words at random to weave together to make a coherent piece of writing, a "found" poem. The only rule was that we couldn't make up any words—they all had to be gathered from books.

When all of us were finished, we read our creations around the table. As we did, we realized that each piece of writing, although gathered randomly from disparate sources, was an authentic reflection of its author, a mirror.

Each evening after the dishes were washed, we'd gather new books for more found writing. By the fifth night our writing sounded like Ezra Pound's *Cantos*, his great long poem in which he orchestrates a multitude of voices.

Our found poems not only saved us from boredom on those cold, rainy nights but introduced us to the possibility of including voices other than our own in our work.

Write a found poem. Gather books, newspapers, magazines, old journals, and first write down interesting words and sentences, then weave them together to make a found piece of writing. Here's an example, from Annie Dillard's Mornings Like This—*a poem she created from directions in a science textbook (*Let's Discover More, *by Samuel A. Thorn and Carl D. Duncan, published in 1957):*

> Break apart stones to see if they contain fossils.
> Break apart a lump of coal.
> Find the Milky Way.

Prayers:
Words with Winged Feet

THE NIGHT after I finished my week of work at the Navajo Nation school, a few of my Native American colleagues and friends wanted to give me a traditional purification sweat ceremony as a gift of thanks. To prepare, all participants had to make prayer ties. Each was given red flannel cloth, to-bacco, and yarn. The afternoon before the ceremony I thought silently of my prayers; for each I placed a small amount of tobacco on a piece of the cloth, tied it into a bundle, and attached all the bundles to a long piece of yarn.

That night, the fire burned outside the lodge. Sparks rose into the clear cold January night, mixing with the stars. We crawled into the lodge—saying the customary All My Relations at the threshold, evoking the ancestors—and hung our prayer ties from the ceiling. We sat silently as the firekeeper outside brought in red glowing rocks with a pitch fork, and placed them in the hole in the center of the circle. The leader of the ceremony began to chant a Navajo prayer; the rocks hissed as she poured water onto them and sprin-kled sage that sparked and filled the lodge with scent. It got hotter and hotter. In the black we chanted and sang, sweat-ing. There were several rounds of singing, and several times, in turn, we prayed: prayers for people we loved who were in trouble or whom we wanted to remember, prayers for people in the world who were suffering, prayers for our enemies. Some of us sang songs we had sung as children. Some of us cried. Some of us were ecstatic. Our silent prayer ties hanging in the dark above us had come to life through our words.

I saw the words rising out of the lodge, into the freezing January night, over the desert toward the sacred mountains, out toward people who were cold and hungry, people asleep in bed, into the universe. That night we believed that words have the power to make something happen.

All writing is in a sense prayer—a sending out of hope, a thanksgiving, a celebration, a song sent into the wind that we hope someone will hear.

Write a prayer. A prayer doesn't have to be religious. It can be an asking, a thanksgiving, a reaching out—a belief that if you send out your words into the world someone will hear them. You can write a prayer about some aspect of your life that needs healing, about another person who needs healing. It can be a prayer of thanksgiving. It doesn't have to be addressed to the traditional sky-god—it can be a supplication to the world. It can follow the tone or the rhythm of a prayer you've heard before if that helps you. Write it, then read it aloud or send it to a friend or tie it up in a prayer bundle—just make sure you send your words out into the world somehow.

Walk

LAST YEAR I fulfilled a dream. I spent the night at the bottom of the Grand Canyon.

The first time I visited the Canyon I was overwhelmed by its beauty—I guess everyone is—the ribbons of red, orange, and yellow rock as far as the eye can see, the light changing the colors so it becomes a new painting every hour. But I found that I was also overwhelmed by something else: I couldn't get near the edge because my knees weakened and my stomach ached when I got too close.

The next day I made a reservation, for a year from then, to spend the night at the bottom of the Canyon at Phantom Ranch. I'd take one year to get in shape for the eighteen-mile hike and to cure my fear of heights.

Suzanne and I arrived at the Canyon one year later. Once again, the layers of rock drew me toward the edge. The hollow sound of the ravens' caws echoed as they glided and soared. As I inched slowly to the edge, I felt the familiar weakening in my knees and my stomach jumped. I thought, How am I ever going to walk down there?

I asked a ranger what the easiest route for acrophobics was. "The Bright Angel Trail," the man said. "But it's hard for me to say, because I've walked all these trails hundreds of times." He tried to reassure me. "You'll be the safest hiker out there because you won't do anything foolish. Most of the accidents that happen are either jumpers or people on the rim who get too close." I was unconsoled but more determined than ever.

The beginning of the Bright Angel Trail is wide. I hugged the inside, trying not to look down the cliffs. I had brought a brochure with me that explained the geological history of the rocks, and I pretended to be passionately interested in geology, my face up against the wall. At the first flat respite, a place called Indian Gardens, the Bright Angel Creek trickles slowly along and cottonwood trees rustle in the wind. We stopped to rest. We still had a long way to go, but I was relieved to have made it down what I thought was the hardest part.

We had continued for a while when suddenly I saw a path the size of half a city sidewalk, weaving back and forth, a wall of rock on one side and a thousand-foot drop on the other. Later, checking the map, I learned that this was the infamous Devil's Corkscrew. I was exhausted. It was too late to turn back. I grabbed Suzanne's arm, put my sunglasses on, and hung an extra pair of socks on each side of them to keep the drop below out of my peripheral vision. Sweating, with an urge to jump to ease my misery, I asked Suzanne to repeat: *Walk, walk, walk.* That's how I got to the bottom of the Canyon, made it to Phantom Ranch. Suzanne's steady voice saying, *Walk, walk.* And I did.

At the ranch the Canyon walls blued in the oncoming dusk, and the stars were thicker than I'd ever seen them. But the next morning arrived too soon.

On the way up again I lifted one foot after the other. For nine miles. Over the bridge suspended above the roaring Colorado River, on trails with hundred-foot drops into the river, back up the Devil's Corkscrew. In late afternoon, when

we reached the top, I got down on my knees and kissed the ground—glad to be back on level land and to have experienced the Canyon from the inside, elated that I had fulfilled my dream, and vowing never to do it again.

Later, Suzanne made a poster for me from a photograph of my back on the trail, me walking, the walls of the Devil's Corkscrew rising above. On it she glued a portion of a poem by Minnie Bruce Pratt:

> I had to make a future, willful, voluble,
> lascivious, a thinker, a long walker,
> unstruck transgressor, furious, shouting,
> voluptuous, a lover, a smeller of blood,
> milk, a woman mean as she can be some nights,
> existence I could pray to, capable of
> poetry.

And one word in bold letters: WALK.

Now each time I think about hiking into the Canyon it gives me courage. If I could do that, I say to myself, I can do anything. I can finish this book. I can write in my journal today how I'm really feeling. No matter what it is, I look up to the photograph of me at the bottom of the Canyon and say *Walk*.

First, describe something you've done in your life that was very difficult: maybe you quit drinking, left a bad marriage, began to exercise daily, quit your job so you could write. Find photographs,

and cut reminders out of magazines. Find a poem or quote and make a collage, so next time if you doubt your abilities you can gather strength from what you've already done.

Is there something in your life that you'd like to do, that feels like the Grand Canyon, but your fears are holding you back? Describe your dream. Make a plan of how you'll be able to fulfill this dream, and try to walk steadily toward it.

Lessons from Art

AT AROUND two o'clock I begin a painting of the barn behind the house. The afternoon light changes so rapidly at the end of August that by five the barn, in bright light at two, is a deep alizarin shadow and the grass has turned a deep forest green. But the first day I paint quickly anyway. There is nothing so lonely as a white canvas of unlimited possibilities. I fill it up with a sketch as I'm working out the composition: the big red barn with its lopsided indigo window, the blue tree shadows on the roof, the pool of green grass, and the pink brick path leading behind. At five o'clock, the end of my painting day, I take a rag with a little turpentine on it and wipe the images out completely, leaving only blurs of the original so I can begin fresh tomorrow. I wipe out the first image, as de Kooning says, "to try to break the willed articulation of the image," so I can gradually begin to layer the canvas with paint, build it up slowly. At the end of each of the first few sessions on a new painting I scrape out and leave only the barest possible paint.

I tell myself out loud, "Georgia, just paint what you see. Don't paint what you think you see." Why is this so difficult to do—to paint what I see? I get into trouble if I think I'm painting a barn, trees, and grass; the stereotypes of what these should look like stop me from really seeing.

By the end of the week, I begin painting the light. There is nothing more satisfying then taking a brush thick with light cadmium red and making one stroke—thick, impasto— over the dulled, blurred red. The paint becomes the afternoon sunlight as it slowly creeps onto the barn and illuminates its whole side. Each evening I hang the painting in the kitchen; as I'm fixing supper or pass from room to room, I look at it and see what I need to do next. When a painting is finished many days have gone by; I've been many hours looking at it and it has been scraped out several times.

When I return to writing, the lessons from art guide me.

Painting and writing are both about relationships. In painting, paint thickness, brush strokes, image, canvas texture, color, and outline all work together. In writing, the words, images, rhythm, voice, and meaning must work together as well.

When I paint I never focus on details—the frame of the barn window, each tree leaf, the dark lines in between the barn slats—until I'm sure of the composition. I begin with broad outlines, then get closer and closer, attempt to render the details more exactly. When I write I start with a draft, a rough equivalent of what I want to say, then revise and rewrite, begin to focus on details.

The piece of sky in the topmost corner of the painting is just as important as the barn. All of it matters, and if I change the color of the barn roof, that will affect the rest of the painting. In writing, every period, every *and* or *it*, is important. Especially in poetry. Every part of a poem will be affected by any change I make.

I try to paint what I really see, to be careful not to make something up to fit the image of how it should look. In writing, I try to tell the truth.

In painting, in writing, I want the images, the words, to

grow gradually. There are some writers who insist on per-fection as the words leave the pen. But this is not my process. Each writer must find her or his process of working; learning another art has helped guide my way.

If you're fortunate enough to practice another art besides writing, you've already noticed the connections between them. If writing is your sole art, seek out biographies and other books about music, dance, or theatre and become inspired by and learn from these other artists. Let the metaphors of that art, the lives of these artists, inform what you're doing.

Blind Contour Drawing:
Revision

IN ART school we sometimes did blind contour drawings. Without looking at our paper, we drew the model over and over, in the same pose, until we felt we had made our hands draw exactly the right shape and angles. When we finally looked down, there were lines everywhere, trails of our attempts to render what we saw; these lines were the corrections and the revisions of the eye. This was one of my favorite exercises. It trained my eyes to look at what I was seeing rather than make up what I thought I was supposed to see.

Writers use words to make blind contour drawings all the time. We call them drafts. Most of the time I haven't said exactly what I want to say on the first try. So I have to go back and see the same thing again.

The true meaning of the word *revision* is this: to see again. No matter what genre I'm working in, it's usually helpful to see more than one time, to probe my initial words. It's not that my first words are not good enough; it's that I need to see again to make sure those words reflect precisely what my eyes and heart see.

There are times when revision isn't necessary. These are

the rare moments when what I write the first time is exactly what I want. I praise the writing spirits when this happens.

I have found that the more I write, the closer my first drafts are to what I want. But sometimes I fool myself. I write something and think it's the best thing ever, only to put it away and reread it later with that sinking feeling in my stomach. My eyes and my mind have fooled me with a mirage.

Divide a sheet of paper into three columns. In the first column, write quickly about something you see outside. Write the first words that come to you. Now without looking at what you wrote the first time, describe it again in the second column. Try to notice more. One way to help probe is to ask yourself questions: What exactly is the color of that fence? What is the light like on that tree? Do this a third time trying to see even more. Read over what you wrote. Was there a transformation from the first seeing to the third? Were you able to notice more the second and third times you looked?

If you find that all your first drafts are perfect, maybe that's your gift—but put them away for a while and reread them later and see if you still feel they're perfect.

Tapping into Words

I WAS trying to hang a heavy antique mirror I found at a flea market and began tapping along the wall, listening for sounds: hollow sounds where there was only air behind the walls, and then a more solid sound when I came across a hidden stud. When I heard the sound of my tapping change, I positioned the nail and hammered it in, confident that the mirror wouldn't fall down.

As I read over words I've written, I tap my sentences in much the same way. Sometimes the sound is hollow—my language is vague or I've used a cliché or the verbs lie passively. The writing there is not as strong as the rest. My first instinct is to get rid of it, cut the weak spot out, throw it away where I will never have to see it again. But I've learned that when I come across these hollow spots perhaps I need to listen harder, put my ear up to the wall again and try to discover what might be inside. Sometimes, instead of cutting the weak part out, I begin to dig; I freewrite to a solid place, a truth crucial to the writing, something I was afraid of and had been avoiding, but there it was, lying just below the surface.

Underline a part in your writing that feels weak. Instead of getting rid of it, write it at the top of a new page: probe it, crack it open. What's the image inside? What treasures might be buried underneath? Or put an equal sign next to a sentence or word that's vague and clarify what you really meant to say.

Punctuation as Spice

FRANZ KAFKA wrote in a diary entry in 1911: "In general a spoken sentence starts with its capital letter with the speaker, bends out as far as it can to the listeners and then returns with a period to the speaker. But if the period is omitted, then the sentence, no longer constrained, keeps flying right out to the listener at full length."

Punctuation is like the brush strokes in a painting. I barely noticed brush strokes until I began to paint; then I'd walk up close to a painting and the brush strokes became part of the expression. If I begin a painting worrying only or mainly about the brush strokes, the images become myopic, can border on being soulless. Instead, I pay attention to the strokes—how thick the paint is, the texture—within the broader context of color and composition.

Punctuation adds texture to language. It's like feeling a fine handmade cloth with our eyes closed; we feel the nap, the bumps, the weave. It's good not to worry too much about punctuation in the beginning. But after a while the punctuation becomes part of what we're trying to say.

Listen to the second paragraph of Virginia Woolf's *To the*

Lighthouse, the long breath of a sentence juxtaposed against a short one:

> Since he belonged, even at the age of six, to that great clan which cannot keep this feeling separate from that, but must let future prospects, with their joys and sorrows, cloud what is actually at hand, since to such people even in earliest childhood any turn in the wheel of sensation has the power to crystallise and transfix the moment upon which its gloom or radiance rests, James Ramsay, sitting on the floor cutting out pictures from the illustrated catalogue of the Army and Navy Stores, endowed the picture of a refrigerator, as his mother spoke, with heavenly bliss. It was fringed with joy.

My high school English teacher taught me never to write long sentences, and she might have asked Virginia Woolf to cut her long sentence into shorter ones, told her it was a run-on. But sometimes writers need to break all the rules they were taught in school.

The first advice I give writers about punctuation is to think of how we learned to dance, to sail, to skate, even to ride a bicycle. There were rules people taught us. And in the beginning, we had those rules inside our heads: 1-2-3, 1-2-3. But we watch a great dancer and we don't see them counting. Dancing and writing are about rhythm. The music of a sentence works together with a period or a comma. Punctuation is an aid to the subtle breath and music of words.

Here is my attempt to imitate Virginia Woolf's rhythm: Walking along the street, a city street, crowded, as those streets are, I saw, oh, so many things, saw a dog lifting his leg against a fire hydrant, saw a white plastic bag tumbling over and over like a tumbleweed before coming to rest, finally, against the thorns of a rose bush, saw a man with a cane, blind, tapping along the sidewalk, his eyes fluttering like the wings of a bird, saw someone's key shining gold against the concrete in the morning sun. Whose key? I thought.

Each punctuation mark is a spice. Spices added to food can make the difference between a bland dish and a delicious one. As we're eating we don't, shouldn't, notice each individual spice. But if I walk over to the spice shelf, open the jar of cumin, and smell and taste it, it is distinctive, pungent, almost soapy. Each writer uses punctuation in different ways, at different times, for different reasons, in varying intensities.

Write the longest sentence you can, followed by the shortest. Listen to the music of the words dictating the punctuation. When you read your favorite writers, become aware of how each has her or his favorite punctuation marks. Reread things you've written and see what punctuation marks and rhythms you tend to favor.

Why Have You Chosen It?

WHEN MARIE and I were graduate students together at Columbia we longed to read women writers who never appeared on any syllabi in our courses. So we posted signs announcing a women's reading group. At our first meeting, twenty women showed up. Over cookies and coffee, we made a wish list of whom we wanted to read: Adrienne Rich, H. D., Djuna Barnes, Margaret Walker, Muriel Rukeyser. These were women with whom most of us were familiar and whom we had even read but never had the opportunity to discuss with anyone else.

We held our bimonthly meetings in tiny apartments that could barely hold us. We were jammed on couches and sat on pillows on the floor against the wall. The first week, we talked mainly about the difficult lives of women writers. What we really wanted to know was how to do it: live, be a woman, and write at the same time. Through our reading we discovered the variety of ways that women coped and couldn't cope with this task. And how through the most dire circumstances women wrote anyway. Because it was a matter of survival. We tried to understand the historical and cultural context within which each woman wrote. We needed models and mirrors with which to look into our futures.

Suzanne recently received a questionnaire, sponsored by the National Endowment for the Arts, researching writers' lives and how grants have affected them. The last question was, "A writer's life is filled with doubt and difficulty. Why have you chosen it?"

"I don't think of it as a choice," Suzanne responded. "Writing is what I've always done. I can't imagine life without it."

Suzanne said that ever since she was eight years old she knew she was going to be a writer. She read the entire Childhood of Famous Americans series, including the lives of Mark Twain, Herman Melville, and Louisa May Alcott, to teach her how to live. She decided early on that she wasn't going to get married, have children, or have a full-time job, because she discovered by reading the biographies that these were things that would keep her from her writing. This was Suzanne's solution, but it doesn't mean that a writer can't have all of this and still write. No matter what your life is like, even if you have a nine-to-five job and six kids, it's still possible to be a writer. Each person must find her or his own blueprint.

One day when I was a girl, I walked downstairs into the living room where my mother was reading the newspaper and said, "Guess what I'm going to be when I grow up: a writer!" My mother looked up and said, "That's nice, dear," but then kept reading. I could tell she didn't really understand that I was serious. Years later when I went to writing school, everyone panicked. "How will you make a living?" they said. My grandmother offered to help pay for my tuition if I became a cartographer instead. "No way," I said. I taught hockey players how to ice skate to help cover the cost of school.

Most writers have done anything they can to pay the rent and make a living, working odd jobs, waitressing, selling books, teaching, just so they can write. The big question everyone asks in this culture is, How are you going to make a living? I know, I have to pay my rent on time. But too few people say to me, A writer! Good for you. That's wonderful! What a gift you will give to the world.

The other day my car broke down on the highway and had to be towed to a gas station. The tow truck driver was born in Turkey and had come to this country ten years ago. He asked me what I did and I said, "I'm a poet, a writer." His eyes brightened. He asked me if I had ever read Nazim Hikmet, a well-known Turkish poet. "Of course," I said. "I love his poetry." Then he began to recite one of Hikmet's poems. The gas station was owned by a man from Rumania. When he discovered that I was a poet, he gave me a big smile and a twenty-dollar discount. In other countries, poets and writers are revered. They still have a life of doubt and difficulty, but they are respected.

It is strange. We know a writer's life is filled with uncertainty but we choose it anyway. It is a matter of life and death.

If you're reading this book, it's probably because somewhere within you burns an urge to write. We writers seldom ask ourselves why we write, but considering the question can often clarify and change what we write. Do you write to make a world in which you can live or for the ecstasy of communion with the great allness? Ask yourself, Why do I write? and fill at least a page in answer.

Finding a True Reader

WHEN I went to writing school one of my teachers drew X's across the poems of mine he didn't like. When I got home I cried. I was too raw and young, hadn't yet developed a strong enough sense of myself as a writer, to let it roll off me or to go to him and say, *This is unacceptable. Being a writer is hard enough without someone's crossing out your writing.* It made me realize how important it is to find supportive readers.

Writers need to treat themselves and their writing very delicately. Only I know exactly how much my words mean to me. And I can guide my readers in how I want them to respond: *Today I'm feeling vulnerable so I only want to hear the good things.* Or: *Be brutal today; I've gone over it and over it, with a fine-tooth comb, and I need a second opinion.*

When it comes down to it my one true reader is myself. I need to be as loving and kind with myself as I would want someone else to be. Being loving and kind doesn't mean not being critical. But I want criticism wrapped in support. The more honest I am with myself about my own needs, the better I can guide my readers into giving me the kind of help I truly need.

Be sure you know how you feel about your writing before you show it to someone else. Write these feelings down first; that way you'll be clearer about its strengths and weaknesses.

Fallow Fields

DRIVING DOWN Scuttlehole and Butter Lane I see the famil
iar strips of green and brown fields: corn, potato, and many
varieties of brassica. It took me a few years to notice that
what grows in these fields is never the same from one year
to the next. One year I'll see a cornfield—tall, deep green,
thick tufts of corn; the next year I'll see the same field with
short green plants and the late white blossoms of potatoes;
then full blooms of purple cabbage; then bare, brown earth,
the field fallow. What little I know about farming has taught
me that in addition to rotating crops, letting the field remain
fallow gives the fields a chance to rest and is just as important. Farmers do not see fallow times as wasted. The earth
may seem barren and unproductive during these rests, but
the farmers know that what's happening in the soil will allow
the fields to sustain crops the next season.

Writers have fallow times too. The problem is, when I
can't write, I panic; I often think of these times as a problem,
a waste. But I keep telling myself that these times are an
organic part of the writing process.

Rilke didn't write for seven years, then walked out on
the veranda of the Duino Castle and heard in his mind,

"Who, if I cried out, would hear me among the angels' hierarchies?"—the first line of his exquisite "Duino Elegies." After a long gestation, that single line began a thirty-page masterpiece.

Reading replenishes the soil for me. The summer I rented a house in Vermont, I often traveled the thirty minutes to the Dartmouth library and by July had two boxes of books overdue. Despite the expense, these books were essential during a time when I wasn't writing. Swimming in the pond, drinking coffee on the porch overlooking a meadow, and falling in love helped too.

If you're experiencing a fallow time, make a list of all the other things you've been wanting to do if only you weren't writing. Here's your chance. The most important thing to remember is that despite the silence something is gestating inside your writing mind and needs to be quiet for a while. In the words of Theodore Roethke, "It will come again. / Be still. / Wait."

Try Woodworking

DURING MY last semester in the graduate writing program at Columbia, a few friends and I asked our teacher Stanley Kunitz what to do when we graduated. He said:

> Do something else. Develop any other skill, turn to any other branch of knowledge. Learn how to use your hands. Try woodworking, birdwatching, gardening, sailing, weaving, pottery, archaeology, oceanography, spelunking, animal husbandry—take your pick. Whatever activity you engage in, as trade or hobby or field of study, will tone up your body and clear your head. At the very least it will help you with your metaphors.

His advice was wise. Thinking I hadn't heeded it, I began to lead writing workshops for children and adults; but through my interaction with people and ages and cultures other than my own I am learning about this country. I've listened to Navajo children talk of the annual January yei' bei' chei' ceremony; listened to poems written by Japanese teachers who lived for years in the internment camps; seen farms and forests turned into strip malls and Virginia battlefields transformed into corporate parks. I've learned about people's lives in rural Iowa, the South Bronx, Oklahoma, and from these journeys I have gathered words and experience that have not only fertilized my writing but have been a great gift in my life.

On every journey my ignorance is whittled away. Looking over a teacher's shoulder or crouching by a seven-year-old's desk, I lose myself in listening; at home, when I sit down to write, I remember and bring all those lands and lives to the page.

What are your other interests and passions? Take something you love to do and make a list of what you've learned from it, of words associated with it. See what metaphors emerge.

What to Leave,
What to Take with You

ON THE last day of a writing workshop in Arizona each of us wrote a list of what he or she wanted to leave behind in that room: shame, lack of time, fear that I'll hurt someone with the truth, fear of failure, fear that no one will really listen to me, lack of support, a professor in college who told me never to write again. . . . Then we went around the circle and shared—adding to our lists as others reminded us of obstacles we had forgotten to write down. Finally, we lit a symbolic bonfire and incinerated all these discarded obstacles. The "fire" raged high and wide.

Next we wrote what we wanted to take with us, what we needed for the writing journey: the voices of other struggling writers, the courage to write the truth, more time, the belief that what I write will make a difference.

Get together with at least two of your writing friends and jot down on small pieces of paper the things that keep you from doing your best work. Then burn these negative messages. Tell them good-bye.

Next, write down the things that inspire and sustain you, and share these positive images with your friends. On the days you feel blocked and empty, open and reread these messages of support and inspiration.

Endings

EARLY MORNING on the last day of writing this book. I'm sitting in my chair, feet up, yellow pad in my lap, as I've done every day for months. I've seen spring pass to summer and summer to fall and fall pass to this cold January day. It has been grey for a week, and snow swirls on the street. Already I feel the sadness, and the relief, of ending. This book feels like a friend's hand I've held for months that I must now let go.

When someone asked the painter Thomas Hart Benton how he knew when a painting was finished he answered, "You know when a painting is finished when it releases you."

I have been released. Maybe now I can read, have friends over for dinner, relax after work, do a little cleaning. I'm tired. Exhausted. For months I've been in this book's grasp. Now my hunger for telling has momentarily been satisfied.

Gloria Anzaldúa quotes a Mexican song:

> My flowers shall not cease to live;
> My songs shall never end;

I, a singer intone them;
They become scattered, they are spread about.

I send my words into the world and wait for whatever new words will come.

BIBLIOGRAPHY

ANZALDÚA, GLORIA. 1987. *Borderlands.* San Francisco: Spinsters/Aunt Lute.

BACA, JIMMY SANTIAGO. 1992. *Working in the Dark: Reflections of a Poet of the Barrio.* Santa Fe, NM: Red Crane.

BASHŌ. 1991. *Narrow Road to the Interior.* Translated by Sam Hamill. Boston: Shambhala.

BLY, ROBERT. 1992. *The Winged Life: The Poetic Voice of Henry David Thoreau.* New York: HarperCollins.

BRECHT, BERTOLT. 1976. *Poems 1913–1956.* Edited by John Willett and Ralph Manheim. New York: Methuen.

BROOKS, GWENDOLYN. 1990. *The Place My Words Are Looking For.* Edited by Paul Janeczko. New York: Bradbury.

CAMERON, JULIA. 1992. *The Artist's Way.* New York: Putnam.

CLIFF, MICHELLE. 1985. "The Journey Out of Silence." In *The Land of Look Behind: Prose and Poetry.* Ithaca, NY: Firebrand.

DELGADO, ABELARDO. 1972. "stupid america." In *Chicano: 25 Pieces of a Chicano Mind.* Abelardo, Barrio Publications.

DE MILLE, AGNES. 1982. "Dance to the Piper." In *Promenade Home: A Two-Part Autobiography*. New York: Da Capo.

DICKINSON, EMILY. 1960. *Complete Poems of Emily Dickinson*. Edited by Thomas Johnson. Boston: Little, Brown.

DIDION, JOAN. 1990. "On Keeping a Notebook." In *Slouching Towards Bethlehem*. Reprint. New York: Farrar, Straus & Giroux.

DILLARD, ANNIE. 1995. *Mornings Like This*. New York: Harper-Collins.

FOX, MATTHEW. 1991. *Creation Spirituality: Liberating Gifts for the Peoples of the Earth*. San Francisco: HarperCollins.

GARDINIER, SUZANNE. 1993. "In That Time." In *The New World*. Pittsburgh, PA: University of Pittsburgh Press.

GRIFFIN, SUSAN. 1992. *A Chorus of Stones: The Private Life of War*. New York: Doubleday.

GRUDIN, ROBERT. 1990. *The Grace of Great Things*. New York: Ticknor & Fields.

HEITMEYER, DORIS. 1994. "First snow . . ." New York: The 42nd Street Art Project.

JUNG, CARL. 1960. *Collected Works*. Vols. 1–18. Edited by Sir Herbert Read, Michael Fordham, Gerhard Adler, and William McGuire. Princeton, NJ: Princeton University Press.

KUNITZ, STANLEY. 1985. *Next-to-Last Things: New Poems and Essays*. New York: The Atlantic Monthly.

LORDE, AUDRE. 1984. *Sister Outsider*. Freedom, CA: The Crossing Press.

MORRISON, TONI. 1987. "The Site of Memory." In *Inventing the Truth: The Art and Craft of Memoir*, edited by William Zinsser. Boston: Houghton Mifflin.

NERUDA, PABLO. 1988. "The Word." In *Lines on the Line: The*

Testimony of Contemporary Latin American Authors, edited by Doris Meyer. Berkeley: University of California Press.

―――. 1990. *Selected Odes of Pablo Neruda.* Translated by Margaret Sayers Peden. Berkeley: University of California Press.

NYE, NAOMI SHIHAB. 1990. "Valentine for Ernest Mann." In *Red Suitcase.* Brockport, New York: BOA.

ORTIZ-COFER, JUDITH. 1991. *Silent Dancing: A Partial Remembrance of a Puerto Rican Childhood.* Houston, TX: Arte Publico.

PALEY, GRACE. 1992. *New & Collected Poems.* Gardiner, ME: Tilbury House.

POU, ALYSON. 1994. "Sunlight shines red . . ." New York: The 42nd Street Art Project.

PRATT, MINNIE BRUCE. 1990. *Crimes Against Nature.* Ithaca, NY: Firebrand.

ROSSBACH, SARAH. 1983. *Feng Shui: The Chinese Art of Placement.* New York: Penguin.

RILKE, RAINER MARIA. 1984. "The Duino Elegies" and *The Notebooks of Malte Laurids Briggs.* In *The Selected Poetry of Rainer Maria Rilke,* edited and translated by Stephen Mitchell. New York: Random House.

ROTELLA, ALEXIS. 1994. "Almost full moon . . ." New York: The 42nd Street Art Project.

SAHAGÚN, BERNADINO DE. 1963. *Nahuatl Proverbs, Conundrums, and Metaphors.* Translated by Thelma D. Sullivan. Mexico City: Estudios de la Cultura Nahuatl.

SALGADO, SEBASTIÃO. 1993. *Workers: An Archaeology of the Industrial Age.* New York: Aperture.

SOMÉ, MALIDOMA PATRICE. 1994. *Of Water and the Spirit.* New York: Putnam.

STRAND, CLARK. 1994. "Back from the mountains . . ." New York: The 42nd Street Art Project.

WHITMAN, WALT. [1855] 1966. Preface to *Leaves of Grass*. Facsimile edition. New York: Eakins.

WOOLF, VIRGINIA. 1927. *To the Lighthouse*. New York: Harcourt Brace and World.

YOILO'I, DON JESUS. 1990. *The Mescal Agave Talks Like That*. Translated by Larry Evers and Felipe Molina. Office of Arid Land Studies. Tucson, AZ: University of Arizona.